CHOOSING A CAREER THAT MATTERS

Executive Coach Reveals
the SECRETS to Finding and Building
the Career you were Meant to Have

Volume 2, 4th Edition

To

THE CAREER POTENTIAL SERIES

By

EDWARD J. MURPHY

CAREER MAKER PUBLISHING

Copyright © 2012
by
THE CAREER MAKER

Published by Career Maker Publishing

10240 E. Tillman Avenue

Mesa, AZ 85212

816.347.0591

ISBN-13: 978-1511864145

ISBN-10: 1511864141

BISAC: Business & Economics / Careers / General

WHAT OTHERS SAY ABOUT
EDWARD J. MURPHY

"I thought I could write a wonderful resume until I had your assistance in preparing a better resume to replace it. I thought I knew how to find a position with a company until you showed me 19 ways to do it. I thought I could handle almost any question until you showed me how wrong I was. I thought I did not need any job interview role-play exercises until you critiqued the results of my videotaped interview. Luck is when preparation meets opportunity. You prepared me and gave me the opportunity to prove my worth to a company. That means you are my luck."

- Roy P., Bellevue, WA

"Ed was tremendously instrumental in directing and assisting the implementation of my career search. It was through his dogged persistence, guidance and genuine encouragement that kept me on track and lead me to the successful position of receiving multiple offers accepting an offer from ...corporation. This was all done in 60 days. Ed was always available when I needed clarification of what I was doing, with recommendations and suggestions as to how to maximize my efforts."

- Jim S. Rancho Santa Fe, CA

"I have appreciated your candor, inspiration, insight and practical experience. I have found your goal identification exercises, negotiation skills, and personal growth strategies particularly useful both personally and professionally. I would most heartily recommend your services as a personal coach to anyone who has high moral character, is intrinsically motivated, and has a desire to be the best they can be."

- Cliff J., Kansas City, MO

I DEDICATE THIS BOOK

TO

My Grandson,

MICHAEL VINCENT PAUL

My MVP!

"Mike, I won't be around during your working lifetime. But if I were, I would tell exactly what's in this book. That's why I wrote it. May it help you and your posterity find and enhance your career. You have so much to give. Make a difference in the life of others, in some measurable way, and you will be richly rewarded in this life and in the next. Much love always."

TABLE OF CONTENTS

INTRODUCTION

"Keep interested in your career, however humble; it is a real possession in the changing fortunes of time.
- Desiderata

This book is about *Choosing a CAREER That Matters* and focuses on how to find and build a meaningful and fulfilling career.

This book isn't about finding a job; it's about finding a place for your career to happen!

There's nothing more stressful than trying to support yourself and your family in a minimum wage job, working two jobs just to pay the bills. I've been there!

It's a SCARY Time!

If you're like most people, you have what I call a Job (Just-Over-Broke). Here you're just trading time for money – just to make it through the month and doing the same thing next month.

Without a career, you'll most certainly experience:

- Failure to develop all your talents

- Reduced total income over your lifetime

- Reduced retirement assets

- Reduced ability to contribute to others

- Failure to achieve your true potential

- Reduced opportunities for family members

- Greater chance of being a "burden" on your family

- Constant worry about not having enough; running out of money before you die

Is this really what you want?

How much longer will you continue your insane behavior; doing the same thing, over and over again, while expecting a different result? There has to be a better way! Well there is and it's time for a change – this is why I wrote this book. I can help you find the career you were meant to have!

One of my clients said it best when he wrote,

> *"Thanks to Ed, I learned the secrets of running a successful job search and in only two weeks I found my career position. I actually had two offers from which to choose and was able to leverage that situation into a 10% raise plus a bonus, all before I ever worked a day. Thanks doesn't seem enough."* – William S., San Diego, CA

I bring over 21 years of experience as an Executive Coach, helping hundreds of people, from recent college graduates to CEO's, find meaningful employment. I worked for four of the largest consulting, outplacement and e-cruiting companies in America in Seattle, San Diego, and Kansas City. It was here that I learned how to help my clients find their True Careers – the career they were meant to have.

Having a career brings these benefits:

- Become absolutely essential to any organization
- Happiness, self-esteem, and prosperity
- Personal fulfillment, making a difference
- Work and life balance
- Goal achievement and financial stability
- Peace of mind concerning your career
- Never having to worry about being a burden on your family
- Better live a blessed life, exercising stewardship over your time and choices

---

Everything in this guide has come from my personal struggles finding employment and the struggles of my clients. I've personally used everything in this book. They worked for me, they worked for my clients, and I know they'll work for you!

This book is unique because it:

- Comes from my personal struggles finding employment and the struggles of my clients

- Teaches you specifically what employers are looking for

- Helps you write and speak in a language every employer understands

- Includes all the things you want to know and the top things you didn't realize you needed to know

- And, much, much, more!

Everything in this book has worked for me, worked for my clients, and I know they'll work for you!

One thing I know for certain, sitting home and waiting for your phone to ring, is the definition of complacency, which will kill your job search and your career.

Stop wishing you were better and do something about it today!

Also, if you feel this information could help someone else, please take a few moments to let them know. If it turns out to make a difference in their life, they'll be forever grateful to you – as will I.

Let's make a difference together – one person at a time!

All the best!

Ed

Founder of *TheCAREERMaker.com*
Coauthor of *The Effectiveness Guide*
email: ed.murphy77@gmail.com

Note: Marked in *Segoe Print* throughout this book, you'll find *Takeaways* or *Key Points* which summarize the main message we wish to convey.

You're not just looking for a job, you're looking for a place for your CAREER to happen.

CHAPTER 1:
WHY YOU REALLY NEED A CAREER

"You control your future, your destiny. What you think about comes about. By recording your dreams and goals on paper, you set in motion the process of becoming the person you most want to be. Put your future in good hands - your own."
-Mark Victor Hansen

What's a Job?

- Job stands for *Just-Over-Broke*

- Trading time for money

- What you do when you just need money

- What entry level employees do

"A career is what you paid for - while your calling is what you were meant for."
- Steve Harvey

What's a Career?

- A chosen pursuit; a profession or occupation

- The general progression of your working life or your professional achievements

- Usually pertains to remunerative (paid) work

Having a career doesn't mean you're locked into the same industry, company, or function for your entire working life.

What's a *Transferrable Skill*?

Transferrable Skills are an ability to do something well, usually gained through training and/or experience, and are the functions you can perform in any industry, at any place, any time.

Transferable Skills are your assets that help you transition into a new role. They ensure your professional resilience and longevity of your career. They allow you to more easily explore other dimensions in your career and acquire added skills and expertise.

While highly specialized skills may be essential to building your own personal competitive advantage, and ensuring success in a particular role or organization, it's your transferable skills that ensure you don't become professionally obsolete over the long term. You have transferable skills that you acquired throughout your lifetime via formal education and training, personal study, social activities, professional activities, and life in general.

While the list of *transferable skills* is huge, they can be consolidated into these categories:

- *People Skills:* Skills that allow you to positively relate to, communicate with, influence, and inspire others like delegating, coaching, listening, presenting, collaborating, and achieving consensus.

- *Analytical Skills:* The intellectual skills that enable you to identify and analyze problems and to find creative, innovative, and feasible solutions like researching, data gathering, data analysis, creativity, and risk analysis.

- *Technical Skills:* The hands-on skills like computer proficiency, the ability to work with specific software, hardware, the ability to build or repair equipment, C++ programming, HTML coding, SQL knowledge, and Adobe suite proficiency.

- ***Organizational Skills:*** The skills that allow you to sort data, plan, arrange projects or resources, maintain accurate, effective, and user-friendly records, coordinate multiple resources or tasks, prioritize, time management, task management, resource management, and coordination, training.

- ***Inter-Personal Skills:*** The skills that deal with workplace character like integrity, dependability, morale courage, good judgment, and treating everyone with dignity, respect, and kindness.

Who should have a career?

Everyone! If you're over 18 and not in high school, you need a career plan.

Do Spouses need a career?

- Absolutely! Something could happen to their other half

- Volunteer work counts

- It's your skills and achievements that matter

- Can you read one book per month?

- Can you learn from the library or internet?

How do careers get interrupted?

Actually, there are numerous ways your career will get interrupted.

Here are just a few:

- Laid-off, down-sized, right-sized, capsized

- Industry disappears (new technology)

- Buy-outs and Mergers

- New Leadership or New Leader

- Divorce, death, poor health, illness, accident, etc.

- Spousal relocation

In tough times, employers must lay-off. They have little choice if they want to maintain *positive cash flow.*

When's the Best Time to look for a Better Opportunity?

- When your industry tanks?
- When your company is bought-out/merged?
- When your company has new Leadership?
- When you have a new Leader?
- When they start laying people off?

Actually, none of the above – because it's too late! The best time to look for a better opportunity is when you're employed!

What are the Benefits of having a Career include:

- Become absolutely essential to any organization
- Happiness, self-esteem, and prosperity
- Personal fulfillment, making a difference
- Work and life balance
- Goal achievement and financial stability
- Peace of mind concerning your career
- Never having to worry about being a burden on your family
- Better live a blessed life, exercising stewardship over your time and choices

Why don't you have a career already?

Some excuses I've heard in the past are,

- I didn't know I needed one
- I thought college was good enough
- I have no time to do anything else
- My Leader will take care of me if I do good work

None of these excuses are valid, nor will they help your career.

What happens to those who do not have a career?

- Failure to develop all your talents
- Reduced total income over your lifetime
- Reduced retirement assets
- Reduced ability to contribute to others
- Failure to achieve your true potential
- Reduced opportunities for family members
- Greater chance of being a "burden" on your family
- Constant worry about not having enough; running out of money before you die

Is this really what you want?

Where's your career right now?

- Can you earn greater income for performance?
- Are you well compensated for your worth?
- Do you get to live wherever you choose?
- Is your work challenging and satisfying?
- Do you have better future opportunities?
- Are you in the right social environment?
- Do you have good job security?
- Is your work balanced with your lifestyle?

You should have answered Yes to all these questions, if you;

- Had a career
- Had a career plan
- Had goals to improve yourself

How stable is your career right now?

The stability of your career can be determined by answering these questions;

- Is my career growing or declining?
- Will my job always be needed?
- Can my job be done by a machine?
- Is this a new or old industry?
- Is there major competition?
- Will my skills work in another industry?
- What technology does my career use?
- Could my career field be outdated soon?

Who's holding a meeting today about moving your career forward?

- Your Leader?
- The President of your company?
- Your Director of Human Resources?
- Your Spouse?

<u>Answer:</u> No one! Unless you do it yourself!

Are you Underemployed?

The underemployed in 2017 are generally those:

- Whose combined family income is less than $40,000 per year
- Who work two (or more) jobs to provide for their family
- Who work more than 60 hours per week just to survive
- With a college education earning less than $50,000 per year

If this includes you, then, congratulations! You're underemployed! Still think you don't need a career?

How soon will you get promoted?

- Is your company doing well?
- Do you get choice assignments?
- Are you popular?
- Is your input solicited?
- Do you have the right skills?
- Are you golden with the grapevine (rumor mill)?
- Have you groomed a successor?
- When is it time for me to move on?
- Have you stopped learning?
- Have you gone about as high as you're going to go?
- Has your status slipped?
- Is your company faltering?
- Are big company changes on the horizon?
- Are you out of the loop?
- Do you dread going to work?
- Is your salary stagnating?

Why is Education and Training so important?

After high-school or college, many people have a negative attitude towards further education and training. The truth is that education and training have little to do with a degree, title, or a piece of paper. Rather, it has everything to do with who you become, who you meet and what skills you develop along the way. The journey is always more important than the destination.

It's all about the process; who you become on the inside as a result of the journey. The character you've developed along the way makes a big difference to business owners. Education and training stretch you to become better; it takes you to task. You must produce a result to pass. You've been tested and found worthy.

How's your program of Personal and Professional Development?

Do you even have one? There's no one on the planet holding a meeting today trying to figure out how to make your life better. If not you - who? If not now - when?

What's your Expected Lifetime Earnings?

According to a 2011 Georgetown University study, here are the expected lifetime earning based on education levels:

Education Level: ($) Lifetime Earnings:

High School Dropout: $973,000

High School Diploma: $1.3 Million

Some College: $1.5 Million

Associates Degree: $1.7 Million

Bachelor's Degree: $2.3 Million

Master's Degree: $2.7 Million

Doctorate Degree: $3.3 Million

Professional Degree: $3.6 Million

Doesn't my experience count for anything?

Absolutely! However, you'll need a lot of it - five years or more. Experience can sometimes substitute for education, depending on the employer. You can still get hired. But, it's just a lot more difficult. This is the reality of today's job market.

Why do Employers hire College Graduates?

If you ran a company and were looking for the best and the brightest people, which group of people would you hire from first?

Group 1: Those tested and found worthy? (College graduates)

Group 2: Those tested and found wanting? (Never finished)

Group 3: Those untested? (No college at all)

If you didn't hire from Group 1 first, then you're probably not in business to make a profit. If you're in Groups 2 or 3, you'll need the influence of your network to meet business owners (or hiring manager) and convince them you can be counted on to produce a result to standard.

In my view, here's the bottom-line on education:

WARNING!!!

If you're;

30-years old without a Bachelor's Degree

or 40-years old without a Master's Degree –

YOU HAVE CAREER CANCER!

Why you ask? Lacking a college education won't hurt you now, but it will after you turn fifty. You may have risen through the ranks as a superstar because of your reputation. But after you turn fifty, all those who knew your reputation have either moved, retired, or died. Now your reputation is gone and you have nothing to show for it because you've failed to improve yourself using the *Road to Career Success (next page)*.

I can't tell you the number of clients I've worked with who had their careers come to an end in their fifty's, including many family members. They all had the same problem; they didn't improve themselves in each of the components of their career. They just assumed that what they had was good enough and they were wrong.

They didn't improve their career along the *Road to Career Success*; Knowledge, Skills, Experience, Achievements, Character, and Balance. And, some let career ending, distractions cause them to become non-competitive in the job market. They made some invalid assumptions along the way that caused their career to disconnect in their later years.

When this happens, you will have no choice but to take whatever job, at whatever pay, you are lucky enough to find. And, you will be thankful for that. You will have little choice but to perform manual labor just to pay the bills and keep from being homeless; not a desirable situation. Idleness and depression will dominate your life. This is not the situation you want to find yourself. And, with a little planning, once a year, you can avoid it.

What are the components of a Good Career?

A good model of your career assets is called the *Road to Career Success*. Let's take a brief look at each component and its definition.

- *Knowledge:* What knowledge do you have? Have you been tested and found worthy? What's your educational level, certification, license, special training?

- *Skills:* What can you do with your knowledge? What're your transferrable skills? What can you do (or have you done) to help enhance your Leader's PCF/BOE goals?

- *Experience:* What different environments (locations, industries, sectors, level, functional areas, size of company, Fortune 1000 companies, etc.) have you been in and how long were you there?

- *Achievement:* How well did you (or your team) perform? What did you accomplish (Results)? What got better because you were there? How did it improve your Leader's PCF/BOE goals?

- *Character:* How do you treat others? True character is right behavior; what you say and do when no one's around including traits like Adaptable, Dependable, Integrity, Judgment, Loyalty, Moral Courage, Positive Attitude, Drive and Respect.

- *Balance:* How balanced is your life overall? Is there anything in your life that is out of balance that could become a distraction to your career later? If you're out of balance, this could be a liability.

This is what you're selling – your assets. Your job during your career is to increase the perceived value of your assets. This is what produces PCF/BOE for the employer lucky enough to have you on their team.

What's included in a Good Career Plan?

A good career plan should clearly answer these questions:

- Where is my career right now?
- Where do I want to be in the future?
- What's my Plan of Action (POA) to get there?
- What're my short term and long-term goals?
- What am I currently working on to add to my resume?

Why do people have career problems?

I can't tell you the number of clients I've worked with who had their careers come to an end in their fifty's, including many of my family members. They all had the same problem; they didn't improve themselves along the *Road to Career Success*. Some let a career ending distraction cause them to become non-competitive in the job market. Others made some invalid assumptions (like their reputation would last them forever) along the way which caused their career to disconnect in their later years.

When this happens, you will have no choice but to take whatever job, at whatever pay, you are lucky enough to find. And, for that, you'll be thankful. You'll have little choice but to perform manual labor just to pay the bills and keep from being homeless; not a desirable situation. Idleness and depression will dominate your life. This is not the situation you want to find yourself. And, with a little planning, once a year, you can avoid it.

What happens to those who don't have a career?

Being underemployed is just trading time for money. This is what happened to those who now need their Social Security check monthly just to survive. This is what happened to some of the homeless people living on the streets.

They focused on just finding a job for 20-30 years, instead of building a career for themselves. This is not where you want to find yourself in your fifties. Or they thought they'd be with the same company forever.

Do you really need more convincing?

CHAPTER 2:
WHAT MUST EVERY COMPANY HAVE TO SURVIVE?

"Never take your eyes off the cash flow because
it's the life blood of business."
- Richard Branson's 21 Survival Strategies
for Small Business Success

Have you ever struggled trying to determine what's most important and what's not; especially when there are too many things to do and too few people and hours in the day to get it all done?

To survive requires focus and prioritization. Many new employers let their employer decide what's most important because they fear making a mistake. However, small business owners, entrepreneurs, and consultants don't have this luxury. Here's a methodology to help ensure your focus and priorities are clear to help you survive.

Here, we'll be examining both Private-Sector Corporations like Microsoft and Public-Sector Organizations like School Districts and Government Agencies, to better understand what's most important to their survival.

What matters most to the survival of
PRIVATE-SECTOR CORPORATIONS?

Have you ever struggled trying to figure out what matters most? If not, you will. Especially, when there are too many things to do and too few people and hours in the day to get it all done. Well, it all comes down to Focus and Priority. But how can you focus or prioritize without knowing what matters most? This is why we'll be examining Private-Sector Corporations like Microsoft to better understand what matters most to their survival.

As an Executive Coach, I often asked senior executives from Private-Sector Companies, "What matters most to the survival of your company?" The first answer I normally got was People. And, people are an important resource, but not the most important resource. Just quit your job and see how quickly you'll be replaced. Some said Technology, which is important, but again, not the most important. So, what really matters most? The only people who don't struggle with this question are Small Business Owners. These guys get it.

Any small business owner will tell you that the correct answer is Positive Cash Flow (or PCF).

Without PCF, the company can't pay their bills and they're soon out-of-business. Without PCF, the company's bankrupt. Game over! And, according to the Small Business Administration, this is the primary reason why 80% of start-up companies fail within their first 3 years. But what about your business unit? If you can link what you and your business unit do for your company's PCF and how it has improved or achieved better results, your business unit is essential to your company.

In the same vein, if your business unit can't be directly linked to one or more of the activities that generate PCF, your unit could be considered non-essential and therefore expendable - not a place you want to stay for long. So, what activities generate *Positive Cash Flow*?

What Generates PCF?

Here are the four most important activities that generate *Positive Cash Flow* for Private-Sector companies like Microsoft:

- **Increase Revenues:** To increase revenues from the sale of products and services normally involves those in sales, marketing, sales support, business development, or strategic development. Can you find and recommend new and innovative ways to sell more products or services like any of these activities? Bringing in new customers, selling more to the same customers, discovering new uses for old products, or finding new ways to bring more money in the door, are how revenues are increased.

- **Decrease Operating Costs:** Decreasing operating costs, or saving money, is everyone's job. Can you find and recommend new and innovative ways to reduce costs like any of these activities: consolidating, eliminating, cost sharing, getting a better price from a supplier, conserving, saving time or being more effective, efficient, and consistent? Because this is how Operating Costs are decreased.

- **Better Use of Available Resources:** Everyone's job is to better use the resources they already have. Can you find and recommend new and innovative ways to better use the resources your company already has like any of these activities: streamlining, eliminating redundancies, consolidating, conserving, waste reduction, process improvement, reducing time required, becoming more efficient, doing more with less, better maintaining equipment and vehicles to extend their service life and finding quicker or easier ways of doing things. And how much money or time could be saved annually? Because this is how to better use the resources of your company.

- **Anticipate Problems Today to Save Money Tomorrow:** Anticipating problems today to save money tomorrow is also everyone's job.

Since law suits are very expensive, can you find and recommend new and innovative ways to anticipate problems today to save money tomorrow like any of these activities: creating important policies and procedures, creating better contracts, ensuring the right insurance is in force, ensuring compliance with outside agencies, creating better physical and cyber security procedures, creating better property accountability procedures, or eliminating unsafe conditions. This is what saves money tomorrow by anticipating problems today.

How can you best use this knowledge?

If you work for a Private-Sector Company like Microsoft, your career depends on your ability to identify, measure, and increase your value added (individual productivity and sustainability) to one or more of the four activities that contribute to PCF.

This step only pertains to half the Job Market. What about all those who are not profit driven like nurses, teachers, fireman, and all those who put themselves in harm's way every day to defend us and keep us safe? Not every organization is profit driven. So, how do they identify, measure and increase their value add?

What matters most to the survival of
PUBLIC SECTOR ORGANIZATIONS?

Since these organizations do not focus on profit generation, what matters most to them is providing a service that serves the greater good (like schools and government agencies).

Public-Sector Organizations use what is called a Band Of Excellence (BOE) to measure and assess their level of services.

For those who work in the Public-Sector, like teachers or government workers, they are required to achieve, maintain, or exceed the *Band Of Excellence (BOE)* set by their organization. So, what is a *Band Of Excellence?*

Band Of Excellence:

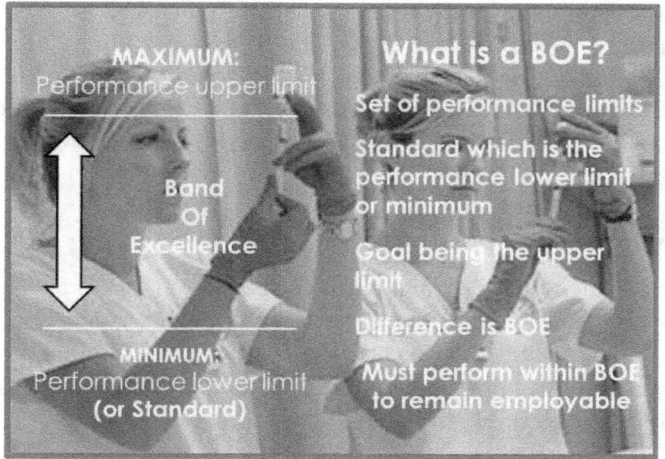

A *Band Of Excellence (BOE)* is a set of performance limits ranging from the Minimum (The Standard) - being the performance lower limit and the Maximum - being the performance upper limit. And the difference between the Minimum and the Maximum is called the *Band Of Excellence*. If your performance stays within the *Band Of Excellence*, you remain employable.

And, here's a simple example.

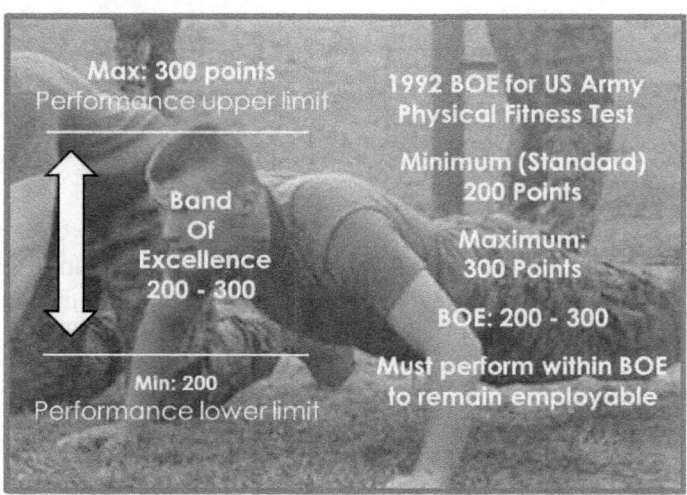

The biggest government agency on the planet is the US Department of Defense. In 1992, as a former US Army Officer, here's the BOE all soldiers used when taking Annual Physical Fitness Test.

The BOE Minimum (or Standard) was 200 points overall. The BOE Maximum was 300 points overall. The BOE was 200 - 300 for the test overall to remain promotable. If a Soldier failed to achieve 200 points overall, he was retrained and re-tested. If he failed a second time, he was considered un-promotable and administratively processed for release from the military.

How does this apply to the Business World?

Let's take teachers and government workers as an example. To remain employable, they're continuously assessed by their supervisors using assessment standards for specific job tasks and behaviors. Employers use these activities to assess both individual and unit performance against their BOEs.

Public-Sector BOEs are measured by daily observations, customer feedback, certification, performance reviews, external audits, visits, compliance inspections, annual qualification, and even continuing education.

How is Performance Measured?

BOE's are used to measure and assess both individual and unit performance, which includes results, behavior, and potential. If each follower continues to meet their BOE Standards, they remain employable. If not, they are retrained, retested and either put on probation, reinstated, or released. And, if they achieve, maintain, or exceed their BOE Maximums, they should expect some form of recognition.

BOE's are needed to measure excellence in Public-Sector Organizations because they're not driven by *Positive Cash Flow*. They are used to make periodic assessments to determine if individuals, units, and systems have achieved, maintained, or exceeded their BOEs. Without a BOE, you can't measure performance or even tell if you're improving or getting worse.

BOEs are also used by Private-Sector Corporations to help generate Positive Cash Flow.

How are BOEs Created?

To create any Public Sector Organization, it must go through these three phases:

Phase 1: Must serve the greater good (schools or government agencies)

Phase 2: Must create a BOE to maintain or enhance that service

Phase 3: Must consistently achieve, maintain, or exceed their BOE

This is how they maintain the funding needed to operate, which comes from city, state, and federal tax revenues. And, if the organization can no longer meet their BOE Standards for services, they run the risk of losing their funding.

If you work for a Public-Sector Organization, like school districts or government agencies, your career depends on your ability to identify, measure, and increase your BOE value added.

Summary: The two things every company in the world must have to survive:

- *Private-Sector Companies* (like Microsoft and all other *For Profit* Companies) must generate PCF and achieve, maintain, or exceed their BOEs.

- *Public-Sector Organizations* (like School Districts) must achieve, maintain, or exceed their BOEs and receive external funding.

Employer's think and speak PCF/BOE.
It's that simple–don't screw it up!

CHAPTER 3:

WHAT VALUE DO YOU BRING TO AN EMPLOYER?

"Price is what you pay. Value is what you get."
- Warren Buffett

Now that you know that employers speak and think PCF/BOE, how can you make your resume speak PCF/BOE? To figure that out, let's first identify your "value added".

To identify your *value added*, here are the most important questions to ask to determine how you're linked to PCF/BOE. Answering these questions will help you determine how you (and your business unit) are linked to the things that matter most: contributing to your Leader's PCF/BOE goals. So, let's review each, one at a time.

How do you contribute to your Leader's PCF/BOE goals?

Here's a true story.

> *One day, Bob was called for a job interview for a job that he really wanted. This new job came with a promotion and doubled his salary. You know the drill; this is where you get the opportunity to justify your existence to complete strangers.*

As expected, Bob was nervous, especially when the interviewer started out by asking him, "Why should we hire you?

After Bob picked himself up off the floor, he stammered something that most people would say, "Well, I was responsible for...."

Then, to make things worse, the interviewer interrupted him and said, "Stop! No one cares what you were responsible for. I want to know what you achieved. What got better because you were there? What was your value added (individual productivity and sustainability) to your leader?"

Unfortunately, Bob didn't get the job, which was a shame because he was the best of all of those they interviewed.

He just didn't know his value added.

Bob didn't know how to sell himself.

This story unfortunately is the norm rather than the exception. All too often good people have no clue what's most important to a potential leader or how to articulate their value added. Has this ever happened to you? If not, it will. But, by reading this guide, you'll never hesitate to answer these questions.

Your value added is quite simply the sum of everything you bring to the table (like your knowledge, skills, experience, achievements, attitude, relationships, character, and balance) that has contributed, in some measurable and significant way, to the achievement of your leader's goals.

You already know how important it is to your career to be able to add value to your leader. But, did you know that most people have no clue how to do that. The problem comes from the fact that few people truly understand what matters most to the survival of their organization.

Once you learn how to identify, measure and increase your value added to your leader, you're well on the way to becoming absolutely essential.

Most people only begin to identify their value added near the end of their career, if at all. To identify your value added (individual productivity and sustainability), here are the most important questions to ask to determine how you're linked to PCF/BOE. Answering these questions will help you determine how you (and your business unit) are linked to the things that matter most: contributing to your leader's PCF/BOE goals. So, let's review each one.

How do you contribute to your Leader's PCF/BOE Goals?

It all starts out with a few assumptions. The first assumption is that you know your leader's goals. If not, ask. Second assumption is that your leader's goals are measurable. And the third assumption is that you (or your unit) contribute directly to your leader's PCF/BOE goals.

What do you (or your business unit) do (what duties do you perform)?

Are your duties essential to the survival of your company? How do you help others and who are you helping? What are you doing to better help others? Most followers don't deal directly with customers. Most often, your #1 customer will be another follower or unit within your company.

What are your PCF/BOE Standards to achieve, maintain, or exceed?

What's the *Band of Excellence?* How do you contribute to your leader's PCF/BOE Goals? Standards here mean the minimum acceptable level of performance (results and behavior). This includes the stated, inherent, and expected standards for the duties you perform. Where's the line between the acceptable and unacceptable? What does your leader and organization expect of your performance (results and behavior)?

How does your Leader measure this?

How does your leader measure your performance (results and behavior)? Who does the measuring? What are the metrics and how often does your leader make assessments?

How does your performance compare to your peers?

Compare to your peers means compare yourself to those at your level within your organization. What are they doing to become better? While this is not the best method for comparison, it's important to collaborate with your peers - because you'll learn a lot.

How does your performance compare to a year ago?

The best way to measure your performance is to compare yourself to where you were a year ago.

Are you getting better over time?

Are you getting better or worse? How do you know for sure? Who is counting or measuring? What are the metrics? If so, how much better? Without measuring and keeping track of how you're doing, how can you ever answer this question?

What do you get for being the best or for improving?

Are there incentives in place for continuous excellent performance? Have you received awards, promotions, raises, accolades, kudos, or other recognition? Do you have copies of this recognition? What was the recognition for? What did you do to earn it?

If you're not improving, guess what your peers are doing?

This also includes professional development, which means additional education, training, and certifications.

What improved because you were there?

From the first day you started, until today, what have you done or recommended to be done that got better because you were there? What was your contribution to moving the work forward? What have you done to make your performance more effective, efficient, and consistent?

Answering these questions will help you determine how you (and your unit) are linked to the things that matter most: your leader's PCF/BOE goals.

CHAPTER 4:
WHAT'S A TRUE CAREER?

"Be not angry that you cannot make others as you wish them to be, since you cannot make yourself as you wish to be."
-Thomas a Kempis

Here it's important to understand the meaning of the term, True Career; the career you were meant to have.

Your True Career is the one that brings you the most enjoyment by doing:

- What makes you feel useful, needed, and fulfilled?
- What's real and meaningful?
- What matters to you and makes a difference for others?
- What you were meant to do?

And, you're authorized to feel enjoyment in your career - that's what makes it your True Career. When (not if) you find your True Career, you'll never have to work another day in your life.

Doing what you like is freedom. Liking what you do is happiness.

To get to where you want to be, especially in the beginning of your career, you may have to do a lot of work you don't like. We're all here for such a short time. Don't waste it. Get out there and find what brings you enjoyment. Then, get really good at doing it; better than anyone else.

Can't I choose a career that pays the most?

Yes, you could. But, you won't experience true enjoyment through money alone. Don't worry about money. Take money out of the equation because if you're doing what brings you enjoyment and you get so good that you're adding-massive-value to the lives of others, people will pay you handsomely to do it for them.

Can't I choose the same career of my parents?

Absolutely, but just because your Father was a Doctor, doesn't guarantee your enjoyment. Do you want to be a Doctor because you want to please your Father? Not a good reason for a career choice because this may not be sufficient motivation to sustain you during medical school and residency. But, if you're doing it for yourself because you want to help heal others – now you've got the beginning of a good compelling reason.

How about choosing a career with the least obstacles?

You'll encounter obstacles along the way in every career. Some are known and some are hidden. They're not there to stop you. They're there to stop everyone else who isn't drawn to the work, not you. Those who find enjoyment in their work will overcome any obstacles. You just don't want it bad enough yet. If you had a strong compelling reason, these obstacles would be speed-bumps and not brick walls. Most people give up because it's too difficult, inconvenient, hard, expensive, painful, too much of a sacrifice, too long, blah-blah-blah! All excuses! Their compelling reason was weak, non-existent, or they let their fire go out.

For example: Let's say your career goal is to become a Doctor, but you have the following obstacles:

- *Obstacle 1:* No money for Medical School. There are many ways to get money for college to include working while going to school. I've known several people who've solved this problem by joining the U.S. Armed Forces to become a medic. Then, they earned their college degree, became a Nurse, Physician's Assistant and eventually went on to become a Doctor. Total out-of-pocket cost - zero.

- *Obstacle 2:* It takes too long. If you truly think it will take too long – you don't yet have a compelling reason. If you did, time wouldn't be an issue.

- *Obstacle 3:* It's too hard. The response is same as Obstacle 2.

It's not too hard; you're just too soft – cream puff!

Ask others for help. What's getting in your way?

CHAPTER 5:
THE THINGS YOU CONTROL

"You may not control all the events that happen to you,
but you can decide not to be reduced by them."
- Maya Angelou

No discussion of awareness will make any sense until you truly understand the difference between what you can and cannot control and therefore influence. What in life do you really control and can therefore change? This simple prayer helped me finally answer this important question.

The Serenity Prayer:

"GOD, grant me the Serenity to

Accept the things I cannot change,

Courage to change the things I can,

and the Wisdom to know the difference.

-Reinhold Niebuhr

What can you Really Change?

In this life,

> *You cannot change other people, places, things,*
> *situations, or circumstances.*

In this life,

> *The only things you can change are your thoughts, words,*
> *and deeds; what you think, say, and do.*

This may be a shocking epiphany for many of you because you've probably spent most of your life trying to control other people, places, things, and situations.

However, until you learn how to truly control that which you can control (your thoughts, words, and deeds), you won't be able to influence others. This may be a shocking epiphany to many of you because you've probably spent most of your life trying to control other people, places, things, and situations. However, until you learn to truly control that which you can control (your thoughts, words, and deeds); you won't be able to influence others.

This concept is so important to understand because Effective Leadership and Followership are about influencing others to do things that they would not normally attempt on their own.

Additionally, most of your future struggles will involve trying to change things you can't possibly change (like other people, places, things, or situations). This struggle ultimately comes down to you trying to change things from the way things are - to the way you want them to be. You'll waste countless hours of time and energy every day trying to change (or control) things over which you cannot change (or control), until you first understand the real meaning and differences between change, control, responsibility, and influence.

This happens because you sometimes confuse the word control with the word responsibility. You think they're the same and they're not! Yes, you may be responsible for your <u>family</u> and your <u>employees.</u> However, you don't control them. You can only influence them. And, you can only influence them after you've mastered yourself; your thoughts, words, and deeds. Thanks to their free agency, they control themselves (they just don't know it yet).

As a Result, you Only Control your…

- *Thoughts:* Attitudes, values, confidence, knowledge, character, prejudices, purpose, passion, opinions, emotions, ideas, tolerations, mood, memory, expectations, values, faith, beliefs, concerns, likes, dislikes, choices, standards, ethics, focus, desires, aspirations, commitment, priorities, goals, perceptions, judgments, prejudices, and stereotypes.

- *Words:* What you say (questions, word choice, following-up, praise, recognition, relationships, counseling, coaching, feedback, asking, persuading, courtesy, respect), how you say it (voice tonality, pause, inflection, tone, intensity, volume, pronunciation, emotion, enthusiasm, and pacing), and what you fail to say (thank you, congratulate, guidance, warnings, corrections = *the Sin of Omission*).

- *Deeds:* What you do (Actions, achievements, performance, behavior, skills, abilities, effort, experience, education, training, habits, your personal presence (handshake, movement, posture, eye contact, dress, hygiene, grooming, gestures, energy, enthusiasm, spirit, and personal space (desk, office, car, and home)), and what you fail to do (help, serve, give = *the Sin of Omission*).

The most important thing you control is how you treat others – even when they treat you badly. Do you treat everyone with dignity, respect, and kindness?

CHAPTER 6:
FINDING YOUR TRUE CAREER

"If money is your hope for independence you will never have it. The only real security that a man can have in this world is a reserve of knowledge, experience, and ability." - Henry Ford

Now that you have a better understanding of what you can control and therefore change, let's examine how and why people really choose their life's work and how they achieve true joy for themselves and others. These 44 Truths will help you find your True Career; the career you were meant to have.

Truth 1: If you knew you couldn't fail, what would you chose to do?

This is the most important question you could ever ask about your career. This is why I listed it as Truth 1. You may not know the answer right now. Your task is to constantly seek the answer throughout your lifetime until you find your True Career. What are you passionate about? Keep searching; it will come. The problem is that people only ask this question once, think they have the answer, and never ask the question throughout their career. This is a mistake. Keep asking this question until you're happy with the answer.

Truth 2: Everything in life that's hard is not always worth it, but everything that's worth it is always hard.

Most people intuitively know that if you want things to change, you must change first. However, they don't make any effort to change. They're waiting for the right time; when their mother-in-law moves out, when the economy turns around, or when the conditions are just right. The truth is that the best time to change is *now*. And, it will take hard work and time to make things happen. You know that improving yourself will be a *struggle*: a stretch, work hard, spending money, spending time learning new things, and looking stupid in the process. Accept it and get on with it. Enroll in something new every year that you can add to your resume. The hardest part of learning anything new is when you first begin.

Truth 3: You can have any career you choose if you have 5 things; a SMART goal, a good Plan of Action, a compelling reason, sincere belief, and a positive attitude.

If you're missing any of the 5 components above, your chances of success have greatly diminished. This, along with taking massive action, adjusting as you go, and never giving up, is the Truth to success. You just must want it bad enough!

Truth 4: Your physical size, age, and gender will include or exclude you from certain careers.

Life's not fair! Truth 3 isn't completely true. There are exceptions. For example, if you want to play football in the National Football League, and you're a 47-year-old, 147 pounds, female – you can forget about it. It's not going to happen during your lifetime. Yes, size, age and gender will include or exclude you from certain careers like being a Jockey or a Sumo Wrestler. Reexamine why you want a career. Based on your physical size, age, and gender, which careers would give you an advantage over others?

Truth 5: Sometimes getting close is good enough.

Using the previous example of the women who had a compelling reason to play in the NFL, what else could she do? Could she become a referee, sportswriter, manager, trainer, agent, score keeper, public relations, marketing, grounds keeper, team doctor, or coach? Sometimes getting close is good enough.

Truth 6: The obstacles you'll encounter are not there to stop you.

The obstacles you'll encounter along the way are *not* there to stop you. They're there to stop everyone who's *not* committed to the work. Are you committed yet? If you are, obstacles won't matter anymore. How bad do you want it? Smash through those obstacles or just find a different way to get there.

Truth 7: If you stay true to what you love, Divine Providence will move on your behalf.

> ***"Concerning all acts of initiative and creation, there is one elementary truth – that the moment one definitely commits oneself, then Providence moves, too."*** – Johann Wolfgang von Goethe

What are you passionate about? What are you doing when you lose all track of time? What are you doing to find it – even if it takes a lifetime?

Here's my experience with *Divine Providence*:

> *I was an average kid by any yardstick; average size, average athletic ability, and average intelligence. The only thing I had going for me was a strong desire. I wanted to serve my country, to protect America, to be a Soldier. My Dad told me that if I wanted to be a Soldier, I needed to go to West Point, the United States Military Academy. So, that was my goal as a 7-year old child.*

> *High school was a real struggle for me. I knew from reading the West Point Admissions Catalog that they only admitted 1000 new students each year from all US States and all allied countries.*

> *Each US Senator could select two candidates each year, and each member of the House of Representatives could select one. From my high school, students that were selected to attend West Point were all members of the National Honor Society, class officers, and outstanding athletes-best in their sport. I knew I had several mountains to climb.*

> *My guidance counselor told me that there was no way I was going to West Point. I didn't have the grades, wasn't in the National Honor Society, wasn't the captain of the football team, or the class president. She didn't even think I was college material. She thought I should learn a trade and go to work in a local factory. Actually, she had just thrown gasoline on the flame I lit years before.*

> *She caused my compelling reason to become a burning desire. I was one of those kids who if you told me I couldn't do something, I got angry and wanted it even more. I knew I had to work harder just to be average. I prayed for help because I knew I could not do this without God's help.*

Each of my four years in high school, I volunteered to go to summer school, not because I wanted too, but because this was how I raised my grades. For any class where I received a grade lower than 80%, I retook in summer school. While all my friends were on summer vacation, I was in summer school, every summer, trying to raise my grades. Every season, I was on a sports team, but my athletic career was substandard at best. But, I kept trying because I knew West Point wanted well rounded athletes.

At graduation, I was ranked 154th in my class of 342 students. In my senior year, I applied to my congressman for West Point, but two of my classmates were selected instead. Yes, they were both National Honor Society members and outstanding athletes. But, I wasn't discouraged. I just needed to find another way to get there.

I decided I needed to take some bold action. I felt that if I was going to become an Army Officer, it might be a good idea to see if I liked being a Soldier. So, in March 1964, I joined the Army National Guard. Four days after graduating high school, I was in Basic Training at Fort Dix, New Jersey. After 6-months, I found that I not only liked being a Soldier, but I actually was good at it. Every year, the National Guard has 20 slots available to attend West Point.

So, my goal was to earn one of those slots. In January 1965, I received orders from the National Guard to participate in Phase II Testing for admission to West Point, which was conducted at Carlisle Barracks, P.A.

When I arrived at the Testing Center, I recognized 6 young men that were a year behind me from my high school. They were the Principal and 5 Alternate candidates from my congressional district. They were all National Honor Society and stand out athletes. This is when Divine Providence moved on my behalf. All 6 young men failed one or more of the 3 admissions tests. None were eligible to attend West Point. Already being a soldier, I easily passed all 3 tests. I was the only one from my congressional district that passed. What are the odds of this happening? I returned home and shared the news with my Dad.

He told me to get in the car and we drove to the office of our congressman. After my Dad explained that I was the only qualified person in his congressional district, the congressman made me his only selectee for admission to West Point.

I share this story to prove that if you have *Divine Providence* on your side, you can't fail. God does answer prayers. Never give up – just find another way to get there. You can do this! The only obstacle in your way is *you!* So, stop getting in your way!

Truth 8: Your True Career will have little to do with the actual work itself.

Hard to believe, but your True Career will have little to do with the work.

Your True Career has everything to do with:

- Who you're serving (your customers, clients, patients)
- Who you're serving with (your Leader and co-workers)
- Why you're serving (purpose, mission, goal, commitment, calling, vocation, drive, motivation, desire)

So, who do you want to serve? The work itself shouldn't be your focus because over time the physical work will change as you progress through your True Career. You'll move from being a doer, to a supervisor, manager, and director of doers. But, who you're serving, who you're serving with, and why you're serving - remains largely the same.

To find your True Career, ask,

- Who do I want to serve?
- With whom do I wish to serve?
- Why do I want to serve?

People aren't in love with the work itself because the work is constantly changing. NFL Football players don't love playing in the freezing rain and snow, getting beat-up, bloodied, injured, or losing the game. They don't love blocking and tackling, lifting weights, being under curfew, traveling all over the United States, living in a glass house – under the constant scrutiny of their coaches, teammates, and the media. So why do they play? Where's the love?

> ***"The thrill of victory and the agony of defeat."***
> *- ABC Wide World of Sports.*

They feel the enjoyment of:

- Winning, victory (recognition)

- Beating someone else (especially someone better)

- Being the best at what they do (recognition)

- Making others happy (fans, teammates, coaches)

- Having someone looking up to them (recognition)

- Doing what they choose to do (freedom, independence)

All their hard work is tolerated, but certainly not loved.

Truth 9: No work experience is ever a waste.

> ***"Bloom where you're planted."***
> *-Mary Engelbreit*

All work experience has a greater purpose. It helps strengthen your character and enhance your awareness. Nothing you'll ever do is a waste. Even if you hate the work, at least you know what you don't want to do for the rest of your life. All experience is meaningful. It helps you better appreciate and understand the people who perform this kind of work, because you've done it before. It also enhances your character, skills, and awareness.

Whatever you do, ask:

- Am I the Best at what I do?

- Do I look for ways to improve at my job?

- Am I improving myself (through education and training)?

If you can answer *Yes* to these three questions, you have a positive attitude, strong character, and are exactly the kind of worker employers are seeking. Or, are you the person who hates their job and does the minimums, just to keep from being fired. If so, you have two choices, *toughen up* and *get with the program*, or do yourself a favor - find work somewhere else.

Choosing a Career That Matters

"What E'er Thou Art, Act Well Thy Part"
- David O. McKay

To find your True Career, work hard where ever you are and do everything you can to improve yourself. Dedicate yourself to finding your True Career. And, in the meantime, do your very best - no matter what! The employer doesn't care if you like the work – they just want excellent results. Can you be counted on to consistently produce excellent results? If not, why would any employer want you on his team?

Every so often I hear people complain about how much they hate their job. They admit doing the minimums just to keep from being fired. What they don't realize is that starting out in any career will require you to do things that are hard, boring, and maybe even dangerous. If this is you, realize that this is normal, necessary, and all part of paying your dues for the privilege to be considered for promotion.

Finding your True Career involves:

- Doing your best work
- Treating everyone with dignity, respect, and kindness
- Making things better than you found them
- Improving yourself
- Continuously producing excellent results

Truth 10: Sometimes your True Career chooses you, but only if you're paying attention.

For some people, their career choses them! It's true. They choose a career based upon what they're good at doing. For others, they struggle to find their True Career. Some people choose the career of their parents because they looked up to their parents and trusted their wisdom. Others choose careers because something traumatic happened in their life that caused them to feel a sense of indebtedness or a sense of connection. It's often hard to explain.

Ask people who love what they do, how they found their career. Sometimes it seems somewhat random and misguided. Be open to that still small voice that whispers to you what your True purpose is in life. Have faith. You'll find your way.

Truth 11: Education and Training are your best Career Insurance Policy.

The area of concentration you select for your Bachelor's Degree matters little. Whether you chose engineering, psychology, or history - it matters little because 65% of working adults past age 40 aren't working in that field anyway. Just get the degree!

Many young people struggle trying to figure out what degree to get in college because they feel they'll be locked into that career field for their entire life. This is untrue! I have a Bachelor's Degree in Engineering and I've never worked a day as an Engineer or built anything. It's important to get your college education, period!

Education and training produce...

Individuals who are more confident and patient, have a greater clarity of purpose, are more optimistic, have greater expectations of success at tackling challenges, have a stronger sense of perseverance to overcome obstacles, are better at problem solving, decision making, creative thinking, quality control, critical reasoning, receiving corrective criticism, meeting deadlines, producing results, researching, collaborating, coordinating, cooperating, written and verbal communications, software and technology, getting along with others and getting things done on-time.

Getting your Master's Degree is a different story. Get your Master's Degree as soon as you can and in an area you really like. And, if you can't decide, just get an MBA, and be done with it. It's that simple! Just get your Masters!

Truth 12: There are only two ways of serving others; either by reducing or eliminating their Pain, or by increasing their Pleasure.

It's true. Think about it. Every career field on the planet does one or the other, either reduce or eliminate pain or increase pleasure. This is why people pay you. These are only the 2-things that motivate human behavior; pleasure and pain.

<u>What Pleasure do humans seek?</u>

Sex, love, recognition, power, reward, food, comfort, freedom, convenience, free time, money, leisure, health, and anything else that keeps them in their Comfort Zone.

<u>What Pain do humans avoid?</u>

Anything that could cause physical or mental discomfort, embarrassment, fear, loss, or anything that could take them out of their Comfort Zone.

In my first career, I chose to protect others (security); this is why I joined the US Army. And, you get to choose. You can change your career anytime you wish. So, what brings you pleasure or relieves your pain?

Truth 13: Dedicate your life to fixing what's broken!

What makes you unhappy? What's broken that needs to be fixed? What social injustice makes you mad? What products or services make you mad? If you want your life to make a difference, how can you contribute and make things better? What problem do you want to resolve? Who or what matters to you?

And, I won't accept "nothing" as an answer. This just tells me you're lazy and haven't focused enough time and energy on a real answer.

Have you ever considered helping people by befriending the poor and the weak, alleviating pain and suffering, righting wrongs, defending truth, strengthening the rising generation, or achieving security and happiness in your small sphere of influence? What's holding you back?

Truth 14: Asking for help is a sign of strength, not a sign of weakness. Not knowing you need help is a sign of ignorance. Needing help and not asking for it is a sign of stupidity.

For some of us, the concept of self-reliance and interdependence are confusing. Self-reliance to some people means doing everything yourself and never asking for help. And, often, our pride keeps us from asking for help; like when we're laid off and looking for work.

Self-reliance is a dependence on one's own capabilities, judgment, or resources. Interdependence is mutual dependence.

Here's another perspective, and hopefully a better clarification, on the subject.

In life, there are three types of dependencies; dependence, independence, and interdependence.

From the moment of our birth, we are all totally dependent on others for our existence. Somewhere in our teens, we think and act like we're totally independent. Then, sometime later in life we finally realize that we can't do it all and we transition into interdependence. Interdependence is the most mature form of dependency.

Truth 15: To be successful, do all that you can do, then asks others for help on things you can't do, things you can't do well, or things you don't have time to do.

To be truly Interdependent requires a higher level of awareness; knowing your strengths and weaknesses, and when, who and how to ask for help. We all eventually recognize our interdependence and realize that goals are best accomplished with mutual support. Time isn't wasted over turf issues or attempting personal gain at the expense of others. So, why is it that every time you lose your job, you try to find a new one by yourself, without asking for help from family and/or friends? Does that make any sense? Are you letting your pride get in your way?

Truth 16: Some will, Some won't, So what, Next?

The fear of rejection (or the fear of asking) is the fear of someone saying *No* is a powerful emotional roadblock to action until you realize that they're not rejecting you as a person, just your request. You may be asking the wrong person, asking the wrong question, or asking at the wrong time. This fear keeps you from asking for help from others. When in doubt, ask! Value yourself enough to get the answers you need to move forward.

Remember, you can't control how others respond to you. However, you can control what you say and how you say it. Not everyone's going to say *Yes*. Every *No* answer isn't a personal rejection. An answer of *No* is only a response to your presentation. It's also an indication of where the other person is coming from at the time you asked. Maybe they need to be educated to a *Yes*.

Also, since asking is a numbers game, every *No* response moves you closer to a *Yes*, especially if you find out their reasons for saying *No*. Don't process an objection as a rejection. Objections are usually a request for more information. You have yet to give them a compelling enough reason to say, *Yes*. This is precisely why the best sales people at the top of their profession finally close the sale (get a *Yes*) only after their fifth *No*. Asking is a numbers game – just ask anyone in sales.

Never give up! Just find another way of get there.

Assess why people repeatedly say *No* and modify your future presentations accordingly. Reeducate them as to the real value of your request. Remember, you have no control over other people, places, things, and situations. However, you can control your thoughts, words, and deeds.

Truth 17: If you keep doing what everyone does, you'll keep getting what everyone gets, and that's not a pretty sight.

Murphy's Law on Life:
"The things that come to those who wait may be the things left by those who got there first."

This is what keeps you in your comfort zone; the fear that you won't be accepted by your peers. This fear keeps you in mediocrity; keeps you from striving for more in life. Some call this complacency, which will kill your career.

Truth 18: If you keep doing what you've been doing and it doesn't work, you're insane!

Have you ever been guilty of insane behavior? We all have on many occasions. Insane behavior is doing the same thing, over and over again, while expecting a different result.

The Truth Test asks:

"How's that work-in out for ya?"

"If what you've been doing is not producing the results you're seeking, then why are you still doing the same old thing?

"Why not try something new?"

"What do you think you need to do?"

These questions will help you come to your own conclusions. This is desirable because you're the one who must execute the solution. If you came up with the solution on your own, you'll be much more likely to take ownership of the solution. If you have no clue what to do, ask for help. But you must decide what needs to be done. Then, commit to a *Plan of Action*, over a specific period, and reassess your results. Then, adjust from there.

Truth 19: Opportunities are neutral. They don't become yours just because you think you deserve it or you've paid your dues.

"Opportunity does not knock, it presents itself when you beat down the door." - Kyle Chandler

Regardless of what you've heard, opportunities don't come looking for you. Find them; go where opportunities hang-out. Then, if your prepared, ready to make it happen, and knock the door down (knock their socks off), maybe you'll get a shot. But, be there - ready to perform. So, prepare yourself, starting today, to knock that door down.

I have faith in you. You can do this!

Truth 20: Your True Career will be the one that brings joy to others by doing what you do well.

Believe it or not, your enjoyment will come by providing enjoyment to others by doing what you do well. Which human problem do you want to help others solve? Every human problem has an entire career field dedicated to the solution.

You've been blessed with special talents to serve others in some meaningful way.

What are your talents? What do you do better than most people? What comes easy to you? What do you really like to do and why? How can your talents help others in some meaningful way?

Truth 21: To find your True Career, find your Compelling Reason.

We're all here on this earth for a reason. That reason will be different for everyone. But, we're convinced that it has something to do with adding-value to the lives of others in some meaningful way. How do you choose to *add-value* to others?

Do you feel a sense of purpose, obligation, duty, mission, vocation, or calling because a:

- Fireman saved you or a loved one from a burning building?
- Priest ministered to your family in a time of need?
- Soldier (your brother) gave his life serving his country?
- Teacher or coach inspired you to become more
- Parent or sibling that inspired you to follow them

You feel a strong desire to give back for all you've been given.

Serving or performing your duty to your fellow human beings is actually one of the strongest forms of love. Have you ever heard of, *Duty to Family, Duty to Country*, or *Duty to God?* We all have. Doing your Duty or Serving demand your dedication, sacrifice, and long-term commitment.

Truth 22: The biggest obstacle to your career (and your life) is you.

You just don't want it bad enough yet. If you had a strong compelling reason, these obstacles would be speed-bumps and not brick walls. Most people give up because it's too difficult, inconvenient, hard, expensive, painful, too much of a sacrifice, too long, blah-blah-blah! All excuses! Their compelling reason was weak, non-existent, or they let their fire go out.

Truth 23: *Where much is given, much is expected.*

If you were born in America, thanks to the 14th Amendment, you are guaranteed the gift of citizenship. America and Canada are the only nations in the world to grant this special privilege. If you get to live in America, you must give back. You have been blessed to inherit the many freedoms that most people take for granted.

If you don't believe me, go live for a year in a foreign country (excluding Canada). When you come home, you'll be glad you're back in the land of the free and the home of the brave. How will you give back? How will you contribute? How will you serve others? Be grateful that in America, at least you have the freedom to choose and to change your decision anytime you choose.

Truth 24: *Self-doubt is a crippling disease.*

The opportunities you let pass always go to someone who had less talent and ability than you. And, the person who seized the opportunity didn't let his pride, fear and a lack of preparation get in his way – like you. Never exclude yourself from doing something you were meant to do. You have all the gifts you need. You can do this!

Stop sitting on the bench and watching life pass you by.
Get in the game! Be a player! Take a risk!

Do you have an *affirmation and a visualization* of your goal? Do you have a SMART goal (Specific, Measurable, Attainable, Relevant and Time limit), a compelling reason, a positive attitude, and a good Plan of Action? What's getting in your way? In most cases, the obstacle is you. Get yourself out of the way. Let go of your fear, pride, complacency, and apathy, and get into action. Stop accepting excuses for not acting.

Choosing a Career That Matters

Truth 25: To find your True Career, do more than expected.

Do More Than Expected

Do more than exist - Live!

Do more that touch - Feel!

Do more than look - Observe!

Do more than read - Absorb!

Do more than hear - Listen!

Do more than listen - Understand!

Do more than think - Ponder!

Do more than talk - Say something!

Do more than belong - Participate!

Do more than care - Help!

Do more than believe - Practice!

Do more than be fair - Be kind!

Do more than forgive - Forget!

Do more than dream - Work!

- William Arthur Ward

Also,

Do more than Observe – Pay Attention!

Do more than Lead – Serve!

Do more than Be There – Get Involved!

Do more than Get Involved – CARE!

Truth 26: You were Born for Greatness! You just don't believe it yet.

This Truth is the hardest for most people to understand and believe. You've been socially and culturally convinced since birth that are lacking in some way. This has caused you to let opportunities pass you by because you either didn't notice, or you thought you weren't ready (or not worthy). This is a sign of fear and a lack of preparation.

Always remember who you are. You are a Child of God.

To help convince you that this is true, here's my favorite inspirational quote from *Marianne Williamson's* book, *A Return to Love: Reflections on the Principles of a Course in Miracles;*

Our Deepest Fear

"Our deepest fear is not that we are inadequate. Our deepest fear is that we are powerful beyond measure. It is our light, not our darkness that frightens us. We ask ourselves, Who am I to be brilliant, gorgeous, talented, fabulous? Actually, who are you not to be? You are a child of God. Your playing small does not serve the world. There is nothing enlightened about shrinking so that other people won't feel insecure around you. We are all meant to shine, as children do. We were born to make manifest the glory of God that is within us. It's not just in some of us; it's in everyone. And as we let our own light shine, we unconsciously give other people permission to do the same. As we are liberated from our own fears, our presence automatically liberates others."

This is how I know you were Born for Greatness!

Truth 27: What you can achieve with the help of others is truly unlimited.

All of us have individual limitations. Some people are stronger, faster, smarter, better organizers, better speakers, or more talented than you. That's just the reality of life. A great example of this is the organization called, Mothers Against Drunk Drivers (MADD). One mother decided that she would no longer tolerate children being killed on our highways by drunk drivers. She united with a few other mothers and the rest is history.

They combined forces to change America's attitude (and laws) about drinking and driving. The size of your cause is not as important as your ability to passionately explain your reason for needing the help of others. You can achieve anything in life if you can inspire enough others to support your cause as their cause. Help enough people get what they want and they'll support you. In reality, they'll be doing it for their own personal reasons. What do you care deeply about? What bothers you? What are you doing about it? You're not alone.

Truth 28: Dreams really do come true, as long as you don't give up on yourself.

"If you can dream it you can do it."
- Walt Disney

Walt had it right! And, if you've ever been to Disney World, you know it worked for Walt. And, it worked for me. I dreamed about being a Cadet at West Point. I dreamed about being a US Army Officer and fighting against America's enemies. I believed it was possible for me. And, I know your dreams can happen for you as well. What're your dreams? What would you love to do, if time and money weren't an obstacle?

Truth 29: You are never completely prepared for anything. Go with what ya got!

"Life has no rehearsals, only performances."
- Unknown

You weren't completely prepared to be born, to die, to get married, to have children, for that job interview, but you did the best you could with what you had. Don't let your fear or pride get in your way. Stand up and take the action needed to move you forward.

If you hesitate, because you don't think you're completely ready, the opportunity will go to someone else. Later, you'll find that the person who stood up and seized the opportunity had less talent and ability than you. What made him different was the fact that he didn't let his fear and pride get in his way. *Go with what ya got and do your best!*

Truth 30: Sometimes your talents and passions aren't things all employers can use.

A young farm boy from Malaysia named *Boey* was forced into arts education because he did poorly in math. Fortunately, he came to America to study animation. While sitting in a coffee shop he started to draw incredible works of art on paper cups with a *Sharpie Pen*. His friends said, *"No one will buy that crap."* But, he persisted.

"The difference between a dream and reality - is just doing it."
- Boey

Today, many of his works of art sell for thousands of dollars. If you want to be inspired, watch this **video** on *YouTube* showing *Boey* using the talents he was blessed with that he didn't know he had. *Boey* happily became an entrepreneur because his talents and passions were not something an employer could use.

Being an entrepreneur includes starting your own business, buying a franchise, buying an existing business, becoming a consultant, doing only contract work, being a temporary worker (permanently), or a multi-level marketing distributor.

Truth 31: Luck is where preparation meets opportunity.

"It's not the will to win that matters—everyone has that. It's the will to prepare to win that matters."- Paul "Bear" Bryant

And, all along you thought luck had something to do with your career success. We don't believe in luck. We know that what others call luck is when preparation meets opportunity. You make your luck every day by working hard and preparing yourself for the future. What education or training are you currently taking that you can add to your resume? Will you be prepared when your opportunities appear?

Truth 32: Good things happen when you go for it.

"Don't wait for extraordinary opportunities. Seize common occasions and make them great. Weak men wait for opportunities; strong men make them." - Orison Swett Marden

Once you commit to do something, and give it all you have, you'll attract the people and resources required to make it happen. It's your passion that attracts others to help you. People love to help others who are up to something; those who have a passion and a purpose.

Your passion releases:

- *Excitement:* The physical sensation that passion arouses

- *Enthusiasm:* Focusing your excitement on a specific purpose

- *Energy:* The power generated by your passion

- *Effort:* Outward manifestation of passion in the form of action

What's your passion? What's your purpose?

Truth 33: During your working lifetime (age 18-65), you'll change careers several times.

This may come as a shock, but it's true. The only way to survive is to continuously strengthen your transferrable skills. Because of emerging technology, products, career fields, companies and entire industries disappear almost overnight. The only thing you can count on is more change – at a faster pace.

The most sought after *Transferrable Skills*:

Led, Managed, Directed, Supervised, Coordinated, Facilitated, Administered, Created, Produced, Implemented, Communicated, Introduced, Presented, Planned, Trained, Designed, Engineered, Prepared, Reviewed, Streamlined, Estimated, Solved, Decided, Coached, Executed, Assessed, and Researched.

Which of these transferrable skills do you own?

Truth 34: Everyone is extraordinary at something.

There are no ordinary people because everyone is extraordinary at something – even you. It's your job to find out what that something is. It's the same with intelligence. No matter how smart you are, you are always ignorant at something. You are here on the earth today for a reason. You are here to add-value to the lives of others in some meaningful way. Be the *Mother Teresa* in your little sphere of influence.

Do small things with great love.

Truth 35: Life will manifest to you whatever you expect.

Life will manifest to you that which you expect. If you expect nothing, guess what you'll get? What do you expect from and for yourself? Is this all there is for you?

"Our destiny changes with our thought; we shall become what we wish to become, do what we wish to do, when our habitual thought corresponds with our desire." - Orison Swett Marden

---

The powers of expectation and desire can help your career. Are you using *affirmations and visualizations*? What do you expect is possible for you during your lifetime?

Truth 36: It doesn't matter where you start, only where you end up.

"Though no one can go back and make a brand new start, anyone can start from now and make a brand new ending."
- Anonymous

It's never too late to start. Age doesn't matter. *Ronald Reagan* was elected US President at age 69. *Nelson Mandela* was elected President of South Africa at 76. And, *Mother Teresa* of Calcutta started the Missionaries of Charity at 40.

Truth 37: It's okay to be unreasonable with yourself!

"The reasonable man adapts himself to the world: the unreasonable one persists in trying to adapt the world to himself. Therefore, all progress depends on the unreasonable man."
- George Bernard Shaw

Raise your bar! Reach higher! Stop majoring in minor things!

Read stories of any great person and you'll find countless example of "pushing-the-envelope", not accepting NO for an answer, ignoring the naysayers, exceeding the limits, going against all odds, accomplishing the impossible; they were unreasonable. Because they were unreasonable, we all benefit from their results. And you can do the same. You don't have to accept second best.

There is no such thing as an unreasonable goal,

just unreasonable time limits you place upon yourself.

You will run into obstacles along the way. Count on it. Some obstacles are known. Others are hidden and won't reveal themselves until the day before you finally achieve your goal. More importantly, the most dangerous obstacles will come from within you. You will lose your courage. You will lose your burning desire. You'll lose your focus and your attitude will change and not for the better. Something will happen to throw you off course.

You'll experience things like accidents or illness, getting married, having children, a death in the family, a job loss, a loss of cash flow, or just someone doing something unbelievable to you that will rock your world.

Never give up your goal, just take a step back, assess what happened, and give yourself more time to move from where you are to where you want to be. Create a new *Plan of Action*.

Truth 38: It doesn't matter how many unsuccessful attempts you make.

Read about the life of *Thomas Edison* and see if you don't agree. Note the number of times he attempted to create the first commercially practical incandescent light. Edison made 10,000 unsuccessful attempts before achieving success. Most people would have quit before 10 attempts. If you continue taking action, assess the results, continuously adjust, and never give up, you'll eventually achieve your goal. It's no longer a question of *IF* you'll make it, but *when*.

Press On
"Nothing in the world can take the place of persistence. Talent will not; nothing is more common than unsuccessful men with talent. Genius will not; unrewarded genius is almost proverb. Education will not; the world is full of educated derelicts. Persistence and determination are omnipotent." - Charles Swindoll

Come on! You can do this!

Truth 39: True failure only happens if you give up or never get started.

Failure is real and sometimes over exaggerated by family members and close friends who are supposedly looking out for your best interest. If you get started, give it all you have, and never give up (just find another way to get there) – you will be successful. Of this, I am certain!

Truth 40: There is no growth without struggle.

"What doesn't kill us makes us stronger."
-Friedrich Nietzsche

Many people think that character can only be developed through adversity. If you grow up without adversity in your live, does that mean you don't have character? Of course not!

That's ridiculous! Adversity means misfortune, hardship, mayhem, tragedy, disaster, crisis, and suffering. Adversity does not include hard work, doing things you don't like to do, long hours, responsibilities, challenges, or obstacles.

However, *struggle*, which is part of life for all of us, includes them all. This is why I've chosen the word *struggle* instead of adversity; it's more descriptive and inclusive. Since there's opposition in all things, *struggle* is what you must go through as a result of opposition. *Struggle* is making a strenuous effort in the face of difficulties or opposition.

Your character is developed as a result of your struggles.

Adversity is only a small portion of your overall human experience and not everyone experiences adversity. But, everyone experiences *struggle* in life. During your lifetime, you'll encounter many adverse emotional situations. Because of the frailty of human nature, you can't avoid *struggle*. And, emotions, both yours and theirs, will play a huge role in consistently producing excellent results.

The struggle makes you stronger.

It helps shape your character.

Let it drive you to greatness!

But, sometimes you get to pick your battles, or at least you'll have some say in the conditions under which the battle will be fought.

Sometimes struggle doesn't build character - it reveals it.

Getting fired (the *struggle*) from Apple, made *Steve Jobs* better. Microsoft made Apple better (via the competitive *struggle* to be the best) and vice versa.

Greatness is not always in what you achieve –

sometimes it's in what you overcome.

Truth 41: Taking massive action is the only thing that counts.

"Success seems to be connected with action. Successful men keep moving. They make mistakes, but they don't quit."
- Conrad Hilton

Wishes, desires, intentions, plans, ideas, attitudes, or goals, don't matter, unless they are followed with massive action! Even if you make a mistake; adjust and keep going. We all want to be as far along in our True Career as our talents and abilities will take us.

Action is worry's worst enemy!

To make this happen, you'll need to;

- Pick a career (Any career will do, initially. Do something! Get started!)

- Work hard to be the best (commitment)

- Consistently provide excellent service to others

- Consistently serve those you work with (Leader and team members)

- Constantly improve yourself by achieving new career goals

- Assess and make adjustments along the way

- Never, never, never give up!

Truth 42: Your attitude is the most precious gift you have.

"The greatest discovery of all time is that a person can change his future by merely changing his attitude."
- Oprah Winfrey

Your mental attitude is the most important asset you have. Here we're referring to whether you've developed and maintained an optimistic attitude concerning your view of the future. It's your way of framing what's possible for your life. And, you control it. Jealously guard your positive attitude towards what you're doing. Many others, with far less talents than you, have gone on to achieve great things with their life. How? They never gave anyone the power to *rain on their parade.*

Don't let anyone *steal your sunshine*. Your future hinges on maintaining a positive mental attitude towards what's possible for you to achieve. It's not your circumstances, but what you do about your circumstances that determine your future. Happiness and success in life depend on how you see the proverbial *glass half full*. Is your glass half full or half empty? It depends on your attitude at the time (a thought). This is a conscious choice you make each day of your life. How do you choose to view your life?

Attitude

"The longer I live, the more I realize the impact of attitude on life. Attitude to me is more important than fact. It is more important than the past, than education, than money, than circumstances, than failures, than successes, than what other people think or say I can do. It is more important than appearance, giftedness, or skill. It will make or break an organization... a church... a home. The remarkable thing is we have a choice every day regarding the attitude we will embrace for the day. We cannot change our past. We cannot change the fact that people will act in a certain way. We cannot change the inevitable. The only thing we can do is play on the one string we have, and that is our attitude... I am convinced that life is 10% what happens to me and 90% how I react to it."
- Charles Swindoll

A positive attitude by itself won't automatically create success. But, the absence of one will surely inhibit your potential success.

Truth 43: Still confused, Serve Your Country!

If you're still clueless about what you want to do, apply to become a member of the US Armed Forces or the Peace Corps. By serving your country, you'll learn a lot about yourself. You'll also strengthen your character and enhance your awareness of the world around you. I've known many bright young people, whose family didn't have the money for college, who applied for a Reserve Officers Training Corp (ROTC) scholarship at their local university.

Remember: freedom isn't free. Someone has to pay for it. If not you, then who? If not now, then when? Find out what you're made of.

<u>Note:</u> The *Price of Freedom* is not American lives; it's *Vigilance.* Someone must have *Boots-on-the-Ground* to create a viable deterrent to evil.

Truth 44: In the end, God determines how far you'll go.

I saved the best truth for last. If you do all you can do, keep adjusting until you find what brings you joy by add-massive-value to the lives of others, you'll be blessed.

However, God decides how far you'll go in your career – not you.

So, relax, do your best, find enjoyment in your journey, and let's see how far this rocket ship called *life* will take you.

> *One day, when Colin Powell was being interviewed, the interviewer said, "General Powell, I have a copy of your college record here, and it shows that you received many B's and C's in your courses. How does someone with this kind of academic performance, become the highest-ranking member of our Armed Forces, the Chairman of the Joint Chiefs of Staff?" General Powell just smiles and said, "It's a great country isn't it."*

Learn the Job Searching SECRETS Employer's Don't Want You to Know.

CHAPTER 7:
EXPLORING DIFFERENT CAREERS

"Your work is to discover your work and then with all
your heart to give yourself to it."
- Buddha

Here's the formula for exploring different careers. I use the acronym, PARTY, which has five simple steps.

To Explore Different Careers:

P: Pick a career field (like engineering, medical, or legal)

A: Ask, why am I interested in this field?

R: What are the Requirements to become a member?

T: Talk to several people in this field.

Y: Can you see Yourself doing what they do?

STEP 1:
PICK AN INTERESTING CAREER FIELD

You have to start somewhere. So, select something that either interests you or you know nothing about. Don't fall into the trap of assuming you know what it's like to be a Firefighter just because that's what one of your relatives does for a living. And, don't ask your uncle what he thinks about you becoming a doctor if he's been an accountant all his life. Big mistake! Why? Because, believe it or not, those closest to you have a bad habit of being "Dream Squashes." They unknowingly only tell you how hard it is to become a doctor because they don't want you to fail.

Use the ACT World-of-Work Map:

The *ACT World-of-Work Map* summarizes and displays basic similarities and differences between occupations. One of the most difficult tasks you'll face if you're considering a career change is to find occupations appropriate to your goals and personal characteristics. You can explore careers by using the *World-of-Work Map*. The map is interactive, letting you drill down to descriptions of specific occupations. It is visual and interactive, designed to engage you in the process of career exploration. Like any map, it needs compass points.

All occupations can be organized according to their involvement with four types of basic work tasks (compass points), working with:

- *Data:* Facts, records, numbers, business procedures

- *Ideas:* Abstractions, theories, insights, new ways of doing things

- *People:* Care, services, Leadership, sales

- *Things:* Machines, materials, crops/animals

Usually one or two of these basic work tasks capture the primary nature of an occupation. For example, editors work mostly with people and ideas. These basic work tasks are the Map's compass points. To help you navigate among hundreds of occupations, the World-of-Work Map organizes 555 occupations into 26 groups of similar occupations (career areas).

The Map serves as a visual bridge, linking you (via career assessment results) to personally relevant occupations. Used together with the *ACT Interest Inventory*, the *World-of-Work Map* can help you see the connections between the work world and the activities you like to do. *The ACT Interest Inventory* can help you as you explore different careers, not by singling out the one right occupation, but by pointing to occupations you may never have considered.

STEP 2:
ASK, WHY AM I INTERESTED IN THIS FIELD?

The reasons why you like or are interested in something are important. However, you may not know you are interested in a particular career because of ignorance; you just don't know what they really do. This is why you should never assume that you know unless you've already served in that career for at least a year.

People often ask me if they should accept a certain job offer or not. My response usually is to only accept the position if they're willing to give it everything they have for at least one year. If not, pass! What if you're not interested in anything? You haven't talked to enough people yet!

STEP 3:
WHAT ARE THE REQUIREMENTS FOR MEMBERSHIP?

What are the prerequisites to becoming a member of this career field? Also, what are the requirements for long-term success?

STEP 4:
TALK TO SEVERAL PEOPLE WORKING IN THE FIELD

Visit those who are currently doing what you're interested in doing and ask these questions:

- How long have you been a member?
- What motivated you to pursue this career?
- What are the eligibility requirements/limitations?
- What does a day in your life look like?
- When you first started, what was hardest for you to do?
- What's the hardest thing you ever had to do?
- What do you like most and like least?
- If you could change one thing – what would it be?
- What kind of hours (schedule) do you keep?
- Do you work on Saturdays and weekends?
- How are you compensated for your efforts?

- Are there any other career benefits? (Retirement, medical, etc.)
- Do you see yourself doing this until you retire?
- In the first 5 - 10 years, what kind of jobs, hours and compensation would a new person expect?

Also, talk to them about your goals and obstacles. Many times, successful people, sensing your sincerity, will help you overcome your obstacles.

STEP 5:
CAN YOU SEE YOURSELF DOING WHAT THEY DO?

Can you see yourself being a member of this career field? If not, why? What's getting your way? What are you resisting - hard work? Hard work is essential to your success in any field, especially in the early years. That's why they call it *paying your dues.* Just ask any doctor how many hours a week he worked completing his years of residency.

Don't be surprised if that number is 80-hours per week or higher. Residents are required to work 48-78 hours straight with little sleep. Is hard work a good reason for judging a career field? What's your elimination criterion? Will you continue to assess other career fields using the same elimination criteria? Keep repeating this process until you find your True Career; the career you were meant to have.

Now, get out there, do your best and never give up!

CHAPTER 8:
THE ROAD TO CAREER SUCCESS

"There are no secrets to success. It is the result of preparation, hard work, and learning from failure." - Colin Powell

What follows in the next three chapters is a series of four self-assessments to help you identify and achieve your career goals. After completing these assessments, you will have a list of your *strengths* and *weaknesses* (your *Career Assessment Sheet*) from which you can build your career goals. Before you begin these assessments, take a sheet of blank sheet of paper and label it, *Career Assessment Sheet*. Then add 2 columns, one titled *Strengths* and the other titled *Weaknesses*.

ASSESSMENT 1:
THE ROAD TO CAREER SUCCESS

Let's assess where you are right now along each lane of the *"Road to Career Success"*, which has 6-components (or lanes); *Experience, Knowledge, Skill, Achievements, Character, and Balance.*

The EXPERIENCE Lane

Definition: What different environments (Locations, industries, sectors, level, functional areas, size of company, Fortune 1000 companies, level of responsibility, etc.) have you been in and how long were you there?

Examples:

- <u>Location:</u> Foreign Countries, Language, Cultures

- <u>Sector:</u> Consumer, Energy, Financial, Health Care, Industrial Materials, Technology, Utilities, Defense, Government

- <u>Industry:</u> Chemical, Software, Entertainment, Petroleum, Electronics, Meat Packing, Food, Fish, Paper, Hospitality, Semi-conductor, Defense, Training

- <u>Level:</u> Entry, Supervisor, Manager, Director, VP, C-Level

- <u>Function:</u> Finance, Research, Marketing, Sales, Manufacturing, Operations, Human Resources, Business Development, Internet Technology, Risk Management, Contracting, Operations

- <u>Size (#Employees):</u> 1 -10, 11 – 25, 26 – 50, 51 – 100, 100+

Assignment: From the above list, select one area that you feel is your strongest and one that is your weakest and record them on your *Career Assessment Sheet* and list them below.

The KNOWLEDGE Lane

Definition: What do you know how to do? Have you been tested and found *worthy*?

Examples:

- Education: High School, Associate, Bachelor, Masters, JD/PE/PHD, or other professional degree

- Training: HVAC, Software, Plumbing, Electrical

- Certification: Project Management, Microsoft, CPA, Security

- License: Law, Securities, Engineer, Construction, Medical

- Continuing Education: Real Estate, Engineering, Legal, Financial, and Medical

- On-the-Job Training: Processes, Procedures, Cyber and Physical Security, Property Accountability, Computer programs

- Books: Your favorite subjects

Assignment: From the above list, select one area that you feel is your *strongest* and one that is your *weakest*. List them to a separate sheet of paper, called your *Career Assessment Sheet* and list them below.

The SKILLS Lane

Definition: What have you done with your knowledge? What are your transferrable skills? What can you do to enhance your Leader's PCF/BOE goals?

Examples:

- <u>Technical:</u> Computers, Networks, Databases, Design, Graphics, Web, Software, Hardware

- <u>Communication:</u> Coordinating, Facilitating, Collaborating, Consensus Building, Presenting, Writing, Negotiating, Persuading, Networking, Motivation, Assertiveness, Non-Verbal Expressing, Active Listening, New Language, Inter Office Politics

- <u>People:</u> Leading, Conflict Resolution, Counseling, Coaching, Reprimanding, Mentoring, Assessing, Motivating, Influencing, Supervising, Respecting, Forgiving, Recognizing, Promoting, Understanding, Giving Feedback, Praising, Goal Setting, Interviewing, Team Building

- <u>Business:</u> Budgeting, Planning, Managing, Organizing, Directing, Training, Meeting Management, Contracts, Profit & Loss, Researching, Creating Systems, Risk Management, Reception, Customer Service, Inventory Control, Physical & Cyber Security, Project Management, Operations, Human Resources, Property Accountability, Decision Making, Problem Solving, Time Management

Assignment: From the above list, select one area that you feel is your strongest and one that is your weakest and record them on your *Career Assessment Sheet* and list them below.

The ACHIEVEMENT Lane

Definition: How well did you (or your team) perform? What did you accomplish? What got better because you were there? How difficult was it? How did it improve your Leader's PCF/BOE goals?

Examples:

- <u>Increased Revenues:</u> How much did you seek? How difficult was it? (New Customers, Up Selling, Backend Sale, Increase Price, New Services, New Products)

- <u>Decreased Costs:</u> How much did you save over a year? How difficult was it? (New Vendor, Conserve, Consolidate, Eliminate, Reduce, Training, Simplify)

- <u>Better Use of Internal Resources:</u> How and what did you save? How difficult was it? (Enhanced efficiency, longer usage, simplify, reduced man-hours, reduce waste/spoilage, reduce Inventory-JIT, Six-Sigma, training, save time, easier, faster)

- <u>Anticipate Problems Today to Save $ Later:</u> What did you do and how much will it save later? (Legal, Contracts, HR Policies, ADA, EO, Employment, Insurance, Protection, Cyber Security, Physical Security, Risk Management, Training, Safety, IT)

- *<u>Band Of Excellence</u>:* Have you (or your unit) achieved, maintained, or exceeded the *Band of Excellence (BOE)* set by your organization (school, agency, or military unit).

Assignment: From the above list, select one area that you feel is your strongest and one that is your weakest and record them on your *Career Assessment Sheet* and list them below.

The CHARACTER Lane

Definition: How do you work with others? What would others say about your people skills? Have you ever led a team? What motivates you? What drives you crazy? How do you respond to situations under pressure? What's important in your relationship with your leader? What do you say and do when no one's around?

Examples:

- Adaptable: Includes flexible, stable, observant, life-long learner, inquisitive, curious, sensitive, approachable, open-minded, considers multiple perspectives, not jump to conclusions.

- Dependable: Includes competent (possesses technical, communication, inter-personal and business skills needed to be effective), efficient, effective, consistent. Intelligent, productive, responsible, reliable, accountable, and follows-up.

- Integrity: Includes honest, trustworthy, truthful, aware, prompt, credible, straight-forward, doesn't play games, responsive, keeps his word, fair, moral, ethical, legal, unbiased, discerning, impartial, virtuous, righteous behavior, and a solid role-model.

- Judgment: Includes assess results and behavior, consistent, anticipates, clear vision, strong purpose, high standards, timely, decisive, delegates, prudent, interdependent, wise, common sense, mature, persuasive, simplifier, organized, balanced, resourceful, sets priorities, recognizes excellence, methodical, thrifty, and sufficient judgment to decide the best course of action.

- Loyalty: Includes obedient, team player, faithful, supportive, fidelity, dedicated, involved, committed, develops team members, and develops self.

- Moral Courage: Includes confident, supportive, calm, firm, persistent, temperate, admits mistakes, apologizes, unafraid, and does what's right.

- <u>Positive Attitude:</u> Includes enthusiastic, positive, energetic, zealous, open, optimistic, imaginative, dynamic, encouraging, team builder, outgoing, contributor, sense of humor, champion, inspiring, motivating, creative, curious, and upbeat.

- <u>Drive:</u> Includes strong duty concept, proactive (takes the initiative), resilient, endurance, diligence, action oriented, passionate, perseverant, intense, future focused, self-starter, problem solver, true grit, willing to take risks, resilient to setbacks, disciplined, fortitude, mental toughness, assertive, sets high standards, risk taker, candid, bold, aggressive, thrives on chaos, embraces change, and makes it happen.

- <u>Respect:</u> Includes forgiving, personable, fair, friendly, civil, teachable, humble, considerate, tolerant, thankful, inclusive, constructive, modest, appreciative, collaborator, tactful, consensus builder, compassionate, helpful, listener, responsive, thoughtful, patient, empathic, understanding, caring, sensitive, attentive, charitable, available, generous, peace-maker, sincere, recognizes diversity, self-control, discrete, and balanced.

Assignment: From the above list, select one area that you feel is your strongest and one that is your weakest and record them on your *Career Assessment Sheet* and list them below.

The BALANCE Lane

Definition: How balanced is your life overall? Is there anything in your life that is out of balance that could become (or is) a *distraction* to your career?

Examples:

- Financial: Taxes, Insurance, Personal Transportation, No debt, Savings, a Will, Retirement, Home owner, 401K, Roth, IRA, College Fund

- Physical: Height and weight proportionate, Non-smoker, Examinations, No stress, No fatigue, Sleep well, Exercise, Balanced diet, Good appearance, Energy, Non-drinker

- Mental: Writing, Reading, Creativity, Curiosity, Understanding, Imagination, Problem solving, Memory, Relaxation, Awareness, Tolerance, Good Self-talk, Slow to anger, Hobbies, Continuous Learning, Confidence, Positive, Optimistic

- Social: Sensitive, Patient, Discrete, Inclusive, Outgoing, Humorous, Listener, Respectful, Manners, Friendships, Contributor, Optimistic, Empathic, Understanding, Attentive

- Family: Vacations, Time together, Moments, Love, Values, Purpose, Acceptance, Encouragement, Support, Structure, Respect, Forgiveness, Role model, Honest, Helpful, Caring

- Spiritual: Morality, Faith, Hope, Charity, Service, Prayer, Temperance, Scripture study, Forgiving, Virtuous, Inner peace, Love of God, Righteous behavior, Tithe

Assignment: From the above list, select one area that you feel is your strongest and one that is your weakest and record them on your *Career Assessment Sheet* and list them below.

CHAPTER 9:
HOW RESILIENT IS YOUR CAREER?

"The greatest glory in living lies not in never falling,
but in rising every time we fall."
- Nelson Mandela

In this assessment, you will gauge the *resiliency* of your career.

Career resiliency is defined as your ability to endure and bounce back from setbacks, problems and/or career interruptions (job loss).

The only way to assess how much risk you're taking is to measure your career *resiliency* by completing this assessment.

ASSESSMENT 2:
CAREER RESILIENCY

Instructions: Select a number (1 - 4); using the legend below, that most closely represents your agreement/disagreement with each statement below. Place your number to the right of each question. When finished, add your total score.

LEGEND:

1 = Strongly Disagree; 2 = Disagree; 3 = Agree; 4 = Strongly Agree

1. My current resume clearly communicates my future potential/value (____)

2. I have written both short/long range career goals (____)

3. I can describe my skills/dependable strengths with success stories (____)

4. I have a coach/mentor who can assist me through a career transition (____)

5. I have good negotiating skills and know what I'm worth (____)

6. I can answer liability questions (no experience, no degree, age, etc.) (____)

7. I have a self-marketing plan developed for my career advancement (____)

8. I have good relationships outside my company with suppliers/vendors (____)

9. I believe in my company's leadership, ethics, and integrity (____)

10. I believe in my company's products and/or services (_____)

11. My skills have changed to keep pace with my profession (____)

12. I'm the best in my company at what I do (____)

13. I have experience in foreign country (includes Canada or Mexico) (____)

14. I recommend cost saving/income producing measures to my superiors (____)

15. I maintain an ongoing relationship with recruiters in my profession (____)

16. I seek out training that enhances my knowledge and skills (____)

17. My pay/benefits (compensation) are above average for my profession (____)

18. I'm challenged at work for my knowledge, skills, and abilities (____)

19. I use a computer daily to produce letters, spreadsheets, and e-mails (____)

20. I am happy with my career and expect to be promoted soon (____)

21. I am active in the association/society representing my profession (____)

22. I've completed education: Assoc=1, Bachelor=2, Master=3, PhD=4 (____)

23. I read at least 1 book per month about my chosen profession/function (____)

24. I have 6 month's salary in savings to cover me during any interruption (____)

25. I'm a good communicator, both verbally and in writing (____)

26. I'm constantly seeking ways to develop myself professionally (____)

27. I have good inter-personal skills and I'm a good listener (____)

28. I'm well respected by my peers, subordinates, and superiors (____)

29. I seek out new technology that makes my company more productive (____)

30. I speak a second language (other than English) (____)

List your total score: ____

By being more *resilient*, you can shorten your recovery time from a job loss, thereby reducing your cost of lost income, enhance your peace of mind, and reduce your stress level. You have no control over your company, your Leader, the economy, or the market place. But, you can control the important areas that you will find from the *resiliency* assessment below.

*Career resiliency gives you greater income producing
potential and a greater competitive edge.*

You'll notice that almost all these statements are within your direct control; therefore, you can change them anytime you choose. If you're not earning the kind of income you feel you deserve, you'll probably want to spend some quality time working with these 30 *resiliency* questions.

- *Score 60 or less:* **Ops!** Your career needs professional help quickly. Find a Career Coach you can trust. Ask friends for suggestions or see your local *Yellow Pages* under Career Development, Job Placement, or Employment for available resources. Focus on the 30-resiliency questions with a score of 2 or less. Create a goal to increase your score for each question. Change the way you think, speak and act regarding your career. It will make a major difference.

- *Score 61 – 90:* **Not Bad!** To better prepare for an unscheduled career transition, review each resiliency statement and select those with a score of 2 or less. Then, immediately develop a plan of action to focus on improving one score at a time until it becomes at least a 3 (Agree). How do you do that? First, you must be willing to change your thoughts and words and commit to taking some bold new actions (deeds). Then, create a plan and take massive action to improve your career resiliency.

- *Score: 91 – 120:* **Good Job!** Begin a program of self-development to strengthen areas with the lowest scores. Since no one is perfect, focus on any score below 3. Get each score to at least a 3 (Agree).

Create a goal to increase your score for each question. If not, you'll have a weakness in your career *resiliency* that could hurt your income producing potential causing some difficulty and stress.

Assignment: From the above assessment, select 3 areas of *resilience* that you feel are your strongest and 3 that are your weakest and record them on your *Career Assessment Sheet* and list them below

CHAPTER 10:
LIABILITIES AND LIMITING BEHAVIORS

"The biggest mistake that you can make is to believe that you are working for somebody else. Job security is gone. The driving force of a career must come from the individual. Remember: Jobs are owned by the company, you own your career!"
- Earl Nightingale

Would you believe that social networking (Facebook, Twitter, MySpace, etc.) could be a liability to your career?

This is because 50% of employers admit checking social networking sites before making a hiring decision.

So, don't post information concerning politics, religion, sex, or humor (includes content and photos). If it's already there, remove it.

A career liability is any discriminator that makes you unattractive to an employer or anything that detracts from your marketability compared to your peers.

ASSESSMENT 3:
CAREER LIABILITIES

Potential Liabilities include:

- No GED or college
- No industry certification or training
- Overweight, smoker, poor health
- Poor hygiene/appearance/behavior
- Bad credit, criminal record (Felony DUI)
- Age: Too old or too young
- Lack of experience
- Inability to communicate your skills
- Not know your transferrable skills
- No *value-added*
- Few PCF/BOE achievements
- Over qualified (too much education or experience)
- Being out of work too long
- Gaps in your resume
- Been in three companies in the past five years
- Previously bad performance reviews
- Lack of good references

Assignment: From the above list, select all *liabilities* and record them as *Weaknesses* on your *Career Assessment Sheet* and list them below

ASSESSMENT 4:
LIMITING BEHAVIORS

According to an online survey of 972 people conducted by corporate trainer *VitalSmarts* (Provo, Utah), many people recognize the behavior that is holding them back in their careers. 97% identified at least one of these career-*limiting behaviors* that prevented them from reaching their full potential.

- Unreliability

- The *"It's not my job"* mentality

- Procrastination and Resistance to change

- Negative attitude and Disrespect

- Short-term focus and Selfishness

- Passive - aggressive tendencies

- Avoidance of risk

Assignment: From the above list, select all *Limiting Behaviors* and record them as *Weaknesses* on your *Career Assessment Sheet* and list them below.

At this point you should have a consolidated list all your *Strengths* and *Weaknesses* on your *Career Assessment Sheet*. If not, go back and identify them. You will need your completed *Career Assessment Sheet* for the remaining chapters.

CHAPTER 11:
YOUR FUTURE CAREER DIRECTION

"What we really want to do is what we are really meant to do. When we do what we are meant to do, money comes to us, doors open for us, we feel useful, and the work we do feels like play to us."
-Julia Cameron

Now that you know where your career is in terms of your *strengths* and *weaknesses*, let's determine where you want to be in the future by determining your *Career Direction*.

Your Career Direction is far more important than the destination because your final destination is not up to you. Therefore, all your career goals should focus on moving you further along in the direction you have chosen for your career.

Here are the components of a good career direction;

- *Title:* Project Manager, Technical Analyst?

- *Level:* Entry, supervisor, manager, director, VP, C-level?

- *Function:* Sales, Marketing, Operations, Finance, Research?

- *Type:* Full-time, Part-time, Contract, Consulting?

- *Location:* Are you open to relocation? How far will you commute?

- *Compensation:* Range, what is your desired pay? Other benefits?

- *Leadership or technical?* Lead people or manage things-accounts?

- *Deal Stoppers:* Things that are unacceptable like 100% travel, foreign travel, exposure to danger, work weekends, etc.?

- *Deal Makers:* What things are a *must have* for you?

Using the format below, on a separate sheet of paper, list on your *Career Direction Sheet* where you are Today in each category.

Sample Career Direction Sheet for Today:

Category	Today	
Title?		
Level?		
Function?		
Type?		
Location?		
Compensation ($$)?		
Leader or technical?		
Deal Stoppers?		
Deal Makers?		

What's your Next Step?

Without a good career Direction, you're nothing more than a *wandering generality*; not a place you want to stay for long.

Ask these questions;

- What's the next step for you?
- Where do you want to be in 3-5 years from now along each career direction category?
- What adjustments do you need to make every year to help you progress along the *Road to Career Success*?
- What are you working on (or should you be working on) that you can add to my resume to make you more marketable?

Now add your answers to the above questions to your *Career Direction Sheet* (the one you completed above) showing where you want to be for your Next Step.

Sample Career Direction Sheet for Today and your Next Step:

Category	Today	Next Step
Title?		
Level?		
Function?		
Type?		
Location?		
Compensation ($$)?		
Leader or technical?		
Deal Stoppers?		
Deal Makers?		

If you faithfully completed this task, you should have a defined *Career Direction,* at least for the short term.

Remember: Retake all four assessments from this book every year to determine what adjustments you need to make to your career.

What are your Long-Term Career Goals?

Let's reflect for a moment on where you want to be long term.

- Where will your career end up?
- How do you plan to use your time?
- How do you plan to balance your work and personal life?
- What's your long-term career goal?

Your career is not a sprint, it's a marathon.
Take it one step at a time.

Here's a suggested long-term career goal. If you have a better one, by all means use it.

"I want to be adding-value to the lives of others and to go as far as my skills, talents, and abilities can take me."

How's that for a long-term career goal? Building your career includes taking care of yourself, your family, and your employer – in that order. Loyalty is one thing, but when Cash Flow is negative, you may get laid off.

In the end, God determines how far you'll go.

And, all along you thought it was luck. I don't believe in luck. I know that what others call luck is when preparation meets opportunity. Opportunities are all around you. The only question is,

Will you be prepared when your opportunity appears?

If you do all you can do and keep adjusting until you find what brings you joy, by adding-massive-value to the lives of others, you'll be blessed. But God decides how far you'll go in your career – not you. So, relax, find enjoyment in your journey and let's see how far this *rocket ship* called life will take you.

Now that you have your *Future Career Direction* and your *Career Assessment Sheet* (with your *Strengths* and *Weaknesses*), you're now ready to create your *Blueprint for Career Success*.

CHAPTER 12:
YOUR BLUEPRINT FOR CAREER SUCCESS

"The greater danger for most of us lies not in setting our aim too high and falling short; but in setting our aim too low and achieving our mark." -Michalangelo Buonarrotti

Your Career Goals emanate from the *Weaknesses* from your *Career Assessment Sheet*. Achieving any career goal involves four Phases: Planning (this Chapter), Preparing (Chapter 14), Executing and Assessing (Chapter 15).

How do you create your *Blueprint for Career Success*?

To set your Career Goals that are both SMART and Personalized, you'll need a *Blueprint for Success*. If you define career success as going as far as you can along the *Road to Career Success*, then what goals do you have to improve yourself in each category; Knowledge, Skills, Experience, Achievements, Character, and Balance (Assessment 1), Resilience (Assessment 2), and Liabilities (Assessment 3)?

Paul Meyer had it right when he said,

"Whatever you vividly imagine, ardently desire, sincerely believe, and enthusiastically act upon, must inevitably come to pass!"

Here are the 8 steps to set and achieve your career goals: your *Blueprint for Career Success:*

Planning Phase:

Step 1: Create SMART and Personalized Goals (Vividly imagine) (Chapter 13)

Step 2: Create a Plan Of Action (POA) (Vividly imagine) (Chapter 14)

Preparation Phase: (Chapter 15)

Step 3: Identify your compelling reason (Ardently desire)

Step 4: Maintain your sincere belief (Sincerely believe)

Step 5: Maintain your positive attitude (Enthusiastically act upon)

Execution Phase: (Chapter 15)

Step 6: Take massive action (Enthusiastically act upon)

Assessment Phase: (Chapter 15)

Step 7: Adjust as you go (Enthusiastically act upon)

Step 8: Never give up! (Enthusiastically act upon)

Now, your goal must inevitably come to pass!

STEP 1:
CREATE SMART & PERSONALIZED GOALS

Is your Goal SMART?

A SMART goal is one that is:

S (Specific): Significant, Stretching, Simple

M (Measurable): Meaningful, Motivational, Manageable

A (Attainable): Achievable, Actionable, Aspirational

R (Relevant): Results-oriented, Resourced, Realistic

T (Timely): Time specific, Time tabled, Time limited

Start by taking one *Weakness* from your *Career Assessment Sheet*. Let's assume that one of your *Weaknesses* was;

No College Education

To convert this Goal into a SMART Goal, follow these steps:

Is your Goal Attainable and Relevant?

To determine if your goal is *attainable* and *relevant* for you, it must pass these filtering questions:

- Is this goal *my* goal (or is it someone else's desire for me)?
- Is it okay for me to put my energy into this goal now?
- Can I fully commit myself emotionally to this goal?
- Can I visualize myself reaching this goal?
- Is this goal in harmony with my values and morals?
- Is this the right thing for me to do right now?

If you answered *Yes* to all these questions, keep this goal on your goals list. Delete any goals where your answer was a *No* or *I'm not sure*. This step is important. Without all *Yes* answers, you'll rarely be committed enough to follow through to completion. And, if you focus on the wrong goal, you'll never be able to produce a compelling reason strong enough to achieve it. Let's assume your goal received a *Yes* on all the above questions. Let's begin creating your SMART Goal statement.

Is your Goal Specific, Measurable, and Time limited?

What specifically are you trying to accomplish? How do you know if you're getting closer to achieving your goal?

Goal: Obtain a College Education.

What's your desired area of concentration? What college will you attend? How will you measure success? What's your desired end-result? This is what a SMART goal statement should eventually look like:

Goal: Bachelor's Degree in Engineering from ABC University (specific), no later than June 20XX (when – measurable and time limited)

The *no-later-than* date above is your graduation date. What does your positive end-result look, sound, feel, smell, and taste like? Describe it in sensory specific terms. Paint a word picture. State the end results in your words. If you do this, it will become more measurable; and, if it becomes more measurable, it becomes more achievable.

Is your Goal Personalized?

To make sure your SMART goal is personalized, it must be *Personal, Positive, Inspiring, and Compelling.*

Make it Personal:

To make your goal personal, it is stated as a complete sentence in the 1st person, present tense; as if the goal has already been completed.

Goal: I have my (1ˢᵗ person and present tense) Bachelor's Degree in Engineering from ABC University, no later than June 20XX.

Make it Positive:

Your goals are stated as a positive, end result using a positive verb like get, earn, own, read, hire, get, live, maintain, buy, choose, or build. Avoid negative verbs like correct, avoid, drop, stop, eliminate, lose, or reduce.

Goal: I have earned (positive verb) my Bachelor's Degree in Engineering from ABC University, no later than June 20XX.

Negative verbs are disempowering. Having a goal to *get out of debt* only focuses on that which you do *not* desire. So, by focusing on *getting out of debt*, this will actually increase your debt and result in producing what you didn't want to happen; more debt. Instead, focus on both saving money and earning more. *Avoidance* goals make your life more difficult. They give *beingness* or *importance* to something that you're trying to overcome. Focus on the positive, end-result you are striving to achieve; like a college degree.

Make it Inspiring:

Add positive emotional modifiers that inspire you. How will achieving this goal make you feel? What emotional phrase can you use to describe how you'll feel after achieving this goal?

Goal: I enjoy the confidence I feel (inspiring, positive emotion) by earning my Bachelor's Degree in Engineering from ABC University, no later than June 20XX.

You can now visualize a better life each time you attend class. Your motivation is directly linked to your emotions. If you feel good doing something, you will continue doing it.

Finally, make it Compelling:

Don't forget to add the compelling reason you're doing this.

Goal: I enjoy the confidence I feel by earning my Bachelor's Degree in Engineering from ABC University, no later than June 20XX, which I know will help me achieve my true career potential (compelling reason).

Now that your goal is SMART and Personalized, you're ready to create your Plan of Action.

CHAPTER 13:
CREATING A PLAN OF ACTION

"Care more than others think wise. Risk more than others think safe. Dream more than others think practical. Expect more than others think possible." - Howard Schultz

To create a good career goal Plan of Action (POA), you'll need to answer a few questions first.

STEP 2:
CREATE A PLAN OF ACTION (POA)

Why do I need a POA?

Did you ever plan something and struggle trying to lay everything out so that it made sense? Having a *Plan of Action (POA)* will definitely help you. Also, a written plan is the first step to making your goal a reality. Without a written POA, you're just wishing it would happen.

What could Delay or Stop me?

Before you start any POA, it's important to take out a blank sheet of paper and label it as your *Issues Unresolved List*: Anything you don't know for certain like Questions, Unknowns, Issues, Concerns, Shortfalls, Obstacles, and Problems (or QUICSOP) that remain unresolved.

The answers to these questions will help you identify what could delay or stop you:

- What do I need to know, but don't?

- What do I know for sure, but the answer is unacceptable?

- What assumptions am I making?

- What if these assumptions turn out to be untrue?

- How will I track all the changes, delegations, and *unresolved issues*?

- Who has already accomplished this goal – recently?

- What problems did he have?

- Have all my shortfalls been identified?

- What are the risks (safety, security, weather, property loss, etc.) and how can they be assessed and mitigated?

- What Questions, Unknowns, Issues, Concerns, Shortfalls, Obstacles, Problems (QUICSOP) remain unresolved?

- How can you resolve all your Unresolved Issues?

Actually, you may not get them all resolved to your satisfaction. Surprised? That's the way life works. Just because a problem is not resolved, doesn't mean your goal is at risk. Any *unresolved issues* that can't be resolved should go on your *Unresolved Issues List*, until the answer is known and acceptable. If the answer becomes available, and if it's still unacceptable (you don't like the answer), keep the issue on your *Unresolved Issues List* until the answer is acceptable.

If you ask how much money is available for this project, and the answer is *None*, keep this on your *Unresolved Issues List*, until this shortfall is resolved. Working to resolve everything on your *Unresolved Issues List* will dramatically increase your probability of success. Don't remove or delete anything from your *Unresolved Issues List*.

You'll need to know all the problems you've encountered, after the assignment. Just draw a line through the unresolved issue to show it was resolved. When you resolve one issue, you'll find that you've uncovered several new issues that need to be resolved. Just add them to your *Unresolved Issues List* and create a POA to resolve each problem. As you create the POA, you will have lots of *Unresolved Issues*. List them all on your *Unresolved Issues List.*

Here's an example of an *Unresolved Issue List*:

Unresolved Issue List				
Date	*Unresolved Issue*	*Who*	*Deadline*	*Status*
~~May 4~~	~~Who is an Aviator?~~	~~Bill~~	~~May 4~~	~~Answered~~
May 5	No money for SAT?	Joe	May 5	On-going
Don't delete anything from this list. You'll need them later. Just ~~Strike Through~~ them when <u>known</u> and <u>acceptable</u>.				

Any questions concerning the POA, that can't be answered, should go on your *Unresolved Issues List*, until the answer is known for certain and acceptable. And, when the answer becomes available, if it's still unacceptable (the answer is still a problem), keep the issue on the *Unresolved Issues List* them until the answer is both <u>known</u> and <u>acceptable</u>.

Working to resolve everything on the Unresolved Issues List will dramatically increase your probability of success.

When one problems resolved, several new problems may be identified that need to be resolved. Just add them to the *Unresolved Issues List*, delegate them to a Direct Report, and create a POA to resolve them.

What are the consequences of not achieving my goal?

List any negative consequences of not achieving this goal. How will *not* accomplishing this goal make you feel? What will you lose?

What skills and knowledge are needed?

What do you need to know, that you currently don't know? Maybe you have no clue. That's okay. Just visit the college and ask current student how they got started, what obstacles they encountered and how they overcame their obstacles.

What people or groups have already achieved the goal you're seeking?

Again, find someone who is going (or has graduated) and ask them all your questions. Maybe, you could even visit them on campus and even audit a class. Can you see yourself doing what they do? What will it take for you to do what they do?

Any other resources needed?

What money, time, and other resources will you need to accomplish your goal? If in doubt, ask! What will it cost you to do it? What will it cost you if you don't do it?

What are you willing to sacrifice, give-up or change?

The bigger the goal, the more you must give up like time, friends, dating, extracurricular activities, hobbies, savings, and your freedom. Just identify them and make sure you're really willing to give them up or to cut back. What are you not willing to give up? Can you say everything?

Why have you not achieved this goal already?

What's stopping you? What excuses are you making? Yes, excuses! Excuses because if any other human being has ever done what you are about to do, there is no good reason you can't achieve do the same. All you have are excuses. You can even achieve things that no other human being has achieved, if your compelling reason is a burning desire. What problems or obstacles have others run into along their way to the same goal? If it's never been done before, gather a group of the smartest people you know to try to help you figure it out. Identify the obstacles and have your contingency plans in place to deal with it if the problem comes to pass. Then ask, *what do I fear? What is stopping me from acting?*

How will you reward yourself along the way?

What short and long-term rewards will you give yourself for doing what you said you were going to do? As you get closer to your goal, reward yourself. Make this journey fun! Reinforce small successes by celebrating them.

What actions must you take?

What actions must you take daily, weekly, monthly, quarterly, semi-annually, and annually? Make a list. Ask how often should these actions be completed to get you to your goal in the time limit that you've set? How are you going to record actions you've already taken? Keep track of your actions and results. Reward yourself accordingly.

What actions must others take?

Remember, you have no control over other people, places, things, and circumstances. But, you can influence others. List what actions other must take and do all you can to influence their actions. Who must help you and how are you going to get them to help you?

Who have you asked (or will you ask) to help you?

Asking for help is a sign of strength, not a sign of weakness.
Not knowing you need help is a sign of ignorance.
Needing help and not asking for it is a sign of stupidity.

The fear of someone saying *NO* is a powerful emotional roadblock to action until you realize that they're not rejecting you as a person, just your request. You may be asking the wrong person, asking the wrong question, or asking at the wrong time. This fear keeps you from asking for help from others. When in doubt, ask! Value yourself enough to get the answers you need to move forward. You can't *control* how others respond to you. However, you can *control* what you say and how you say it. Not everyone's going to say *Yes*. Every *No* isn't a personal rejection. An answer of *No* is only a response to your presentation.

It's also an indication of where the other person is coming from at the time you asked. Maybe they need to be educated to a *Yes*. Also, since asking is a numbers game, every *No* response moves you closer to a *Yes*, especially if you find out their reasons for saying *No*. Don't process an objection as a rejection. Objections are usually a request for more information. You have yet to give them a compelling enough reason to say, *Yes*. This is precisely why the best sales people at the top of their profession finally close the sale (get a *Yes*) only after receiving their fifth *No*.

Asking is a numbers game – just ask anyone in sales.
They'll tell you, "Some will, Some won't, So what, Next."
Keep going! Don't let rejection stop you!

Assess why people repeatedly say *No* and modify your future presentations accordingly. Reeducate them as to the real value of your request. You have no control over other people, places, things, and situations. However, you can control your thoughts, words, and deeds.

What are your tasks and key dates?

A task is anything that needs to be accomplished so that your goal is achieved. A key date (or milestone) is merely an event (start or finish) associated with a specific calendar date. Your key date is graduation (finish), but you need other key dates along the way to measure your progress. Can your goal be broken down into phases? Of course! Does the *"Going to college"* goal have time phases? When will each phase start and end? As you do this, you're setting your key date (milestones).

What's your Time table?

A Time table is a table listing all your tasks and the key dates (in sequential order), showing the four phases of any goal; Planning, Preparing, Executing, and Assessing. Your Time table is your *desired* or *planned* path. You can now compare your *desired* path to where you *actually* are in terms of achieving your goal. Are you on schedule? The example Time table below assumes that you have already graduated for High School and are employed out in the workforce.

Sample Time Table for Going to College:

Phase   Date   Action Step (Task)

Planning Phase:

(Date) Set Goal

(_____) Complete Plan of Action

(_____) Take SAT/ACTs

(_____) Apply to colleges

Preparing Phase:

(_____) Obtain funding (Scholarship/Employer)

(_____) Visit colleges

Executing Phase:

(_____) Begin Freshman Year

(_____) Begin Sophomore year

(_____) Begin Junior year

(_____) Begin Senior year

(_____) Graduation

Using the backwards planning process, along with a Time table, allows you to take maximum advantage of whatever time you have left, prior to starting your goal, to complete all necessary tasks. A Time table also shows the sequencing of <u>key dates</u> and <u>tasks</u> (by Phase) that need to be completed during each phase. As the above Time table shows, your first key date is *"Set Goals"* and the last key date is *"Graduation"*.

To whom will you report your actions and results?

Being prepared to verbalize your progress toward your goal means that you are ready to accept full responsibility and bring others into your goal. Sharing your goals with another person makes you accountable and allows the other person to give you honest feedback, advice, and information so you can go further. Be careful whom you select and make sure it is a person who can guide you with support and encouragement.

What's your Plan of Action (POA)?

If you've captured all the answers to the questions in this chapter, you already have your POA. Congratulations! Create a written goal plan in preparation for talking with another person. The real benefit of the POA is to help you think through all the Planning and Preparing requirements for your goal and how you'll achieve each one.

Are you ahead or behind schedule according to your Time table? Have you thought of everything? Putting you goal POA on paper is your personal commitment to action. When ready, review your POA with another person. This is just one example of a POA for one goal. Use this chapter as your template to help you create your POA for all your goals. Now your Plan of Action is ready for your career goal, it's time to move to Phase 2, Preparation.

CHAPTER 14:
ACHIEVING A FULFILLING CAREER

"We live in a culture that relishes tearing others down. It's ultimately more fulfilling, though, to help people reach their goals. Instead of feeling jealous, remember: If God did it for them, He can do it for you."
- Joel Osteen

Once your Plan of Action is done, you're finished with the *Planning Phase*. You're now ready to begin the *Preparation Phase* of achieving your goal.

STEP 3:
IDENTIFY YOUR COMPELLING REASON

The stronger your compelling reason, the greater your probability of success. That's right, if you want to increase your chances of achieving your goal, you'll need a compelling reason. Why do you want this goal? What's in it for you? How will you benefit or be rewarded? Desire is a sense of hoping for an outcome. Desire is the fire that sets action aflame. When you desire something, you're excited by the thought of achieving your goal, and you'll want to take actions to obtain it.

Human desire is the fundamental motivation of all human action. A goal normally goes through several stages before it becomes a *burning desire*. First, your goal may start out as curiosity. Over time, after studying your goal, it turns into a good reason. Then, as time passes it could become a compelling reason. Eventually, if you keep your focus, it'll become a desire. And, if you're really blessed, it'll become a *burning desire*.

What's a Burning Desire?

A *burning desire* is more than a wish or a want or a dream. Wishes, wants and dreams typically are self-generated. However, a burning desire is something that comes from your Spirit. Your Best self is compelling you toward something. A *burning desire* is what animates your purpose and values. One day your Best self will speak up and you'll no longer be able to tolerate staying in your Comfort Zone.

The truth is that everyone has a burning desire. It's already inside you. You just need to find it and let it out.

Eventually, your *burning desire* won't be an option anymore. The time will arrive. This is when you'll need a POA, gather all your courage, and step in the direction of your desire. Gradually, your *burning desire* will provide the motivation to achieve your purpose.

When your purpose is animated by desire that truly burns, it doesn't mean your journey will be any easier. It just means that the outcome will become more certain.

All I had going for me as a kid, and throughout my life, was a *burning desire* to work harder than anyone else and to not give up or give in until I won. No excuses, no whining!

I'm living witness that if you prepare yourself, do all that you can do towards achieving a righteous goal, Divine Providence will move on your behalf.

Why is a burning desire so important?

Live your life with no excuses, no complaints, and no regrets!!

A *burning desire* ensures that you will continue:

- Giving it all you have
- Getting up after being knocked down
- Finding new ways to overcome challenges
- Your commitment to see it through to a successful completion

STEP 4:
MAINTAIN YOUR SINCERE BELIEF

Life will manifest to you whatever you expect. If you expect nothing, guess what you'll get? All of us have individual limitations.

> *You've been given special gifts and blessings. What you do with your gifts will determine your destiny.*

What are your special gifts and how can you use them to affect the lives of others in some meaningful way? Are you using *Affirmations and Visualizations* to help you maintain your sincere beliefs? What's holding you back?

Are you Committed to Purpose?

Commitment is a duty, obligation or responsibility, a promise or agreement to do something in the future; being bound emotionally or intellectually to a course of action or to another person. People who've committed to purpose do their best and get things done, are happy and lucky just to have a job, are looking for things that are right, don't complain or gossip, ask for input and feedback from others, and take personal responsibility for their actions and the results. Does this describe you?

> *Committing to purpose is the most powerful, life altering concept I know of that can truly change your life.*
> *So, how can you become committed to purpose?*

Committing to purpose is mentally accepting your situation and making the best of it. Your purpose comes from letting go of your need to question, complain, or argue and to move toward total cooperation. You are *all in* and there is no turning back. An excellent example is *Mother Teresa*. She didn't complain about having to work in the slums of Calcutta.

She accepted her situation and did the best she could to ease the pain and suffering - one soul at a time. She was in an impossible situation that she knew she couldn't change. So, she accepted it, *committed to purpose,* and did the best she could. Commitment requires action. You can say you're committed, but the proof is in what you've done. Commitment means that you've *"burned your bridges"* so there's no going back.

How can you know if you're Committed?

You're committed when you've:

- Let go of all the negatives that have been holding you back

- Completely accepted who you are and what you're doing

- Disengaged from your struggles and no longer question or complain

- Forgotten about yourself and resolved to fully cooperate – without hesitation or reservation

When this happens, you've arrived; you've *committed to purpose.*

STEP 5:
MAINTAIN YOUR POSITIVE ATTITUDE

Start by adopt an attitude of gratitude in all you do. Count your blessings daily. Look back on your life and review your accomplishments. Now, compare whatever obstacle lies before you with all your past accomplishments. See how the obstacle or challenge, which was a formidable mountain, has shrunk to be nothing more than a speed bump.

Your positive attitude is the most important asset you have.

Here we're referring to whether you've developed and maintained an optimistic attitude concerning your view of your future. It's your way of framing what's possible for your life. And, you control it. Jealously guard your positive attitude towards what you're doing. Many others, with far less talents than you, have gone on to achieve great things with their life. How?

They never gave anyone the power to *rain-on-their-parade*. Don't let anyone *steal your sunshine*. Your career hinges on maintaining a positive attitude towards what's possible for you. It's not your circumstances, but what you do about your circumstances that determine your future. Now that you've completed steps 3-5, you're now ready to begin the *Execution Phase* of achieving your goal.

STEP 6:
TAKE MASSIVE ACTION!

Your POA is done and it's time to start taking the actions steps listed on your Time table.

What's your next step?

Massive action means, get it done today! Make it happen!
Do not go to bed until it's done!

Tomorrow, start preparing for the next action step. Get it done! Work towards your goal every day. Use your *affirmation and visualization* every day. Talk to people who have done what you intend to do. *Pull-out-all-the-stops*! Keep going! Since you're in the *Execution Phase*, Step 6, you're now ready to begin the *Assessment Phase* of achieving your goal.

STEP 7:
ADJUST AS YOU GO

Most people think a compass needle always points to *True North*. This is false. A compass needle always points to *Magnetic North*. To find *True North*, you need to adjust by either adding or subtracting the declination constant for your location. Your career goals are much the same way.

If you intend to continuously experience joy,
constantly adjust your career.

These adjustments include periodic:

- Assessments (measuring)
- Appraisals (feedback from your Leader and team members)
- New education
- New training and certification
- New challenges (stepping outside your Comfort Zone)

Guard against complacency because it will kill your career.

What if I run into obstacles?

You will run into obstacles along the way. Count on it. Some obstacles are known. Others are hidden and won't reveal themselves until the day before you finally achieve your goal.

The most dangerous obstacles lie between your ears.

Your obstacles include:

- Failure to accept personal responsibility for your actions and the results
- Losing your compelling reason
- Letting an obstacle stop you
- Letting your negative emotions stop you
- Failure to work your plan
- Failure to adjust your plan, as needed
- Failure to give yourself more time

Things will happen to throw you off course, like accidents, failure, illness, getting married, having children, or a death in the family.

Remember, failure only happens if you quit!

Now what? Pick up the pieces and keep going! Use these obstacles to strengthen you and drive you to greatness.

STEP 8:
NEVER GIVE UP

Never give up - just find another way to get there.

Don't give up your goal, just take a step back, assess what happened, and give yourself more time to move from where you are to where you want to be. Create a new Time table.

There is no such thing as an unreasonable goal, just unreasonable time limits we place upon ourselves.

Who else has accomplished this goal? Can they recommend other ways to overcome your obstacles? Ask others for help. Never give up!

What if I never reach my goal?

Follow this example. Pretend your goal was to achieve a net worth of $1 Million by the time you were 60, so you could comfortably retire. If on your 60th birthday you assessed your net worth and it was only $900,000, would you be sad? Would you consider yourself a failure? You must be a failure if you didn't reach your goal, right?

Here's the *only* important question to ask,

What would your net worth be today, without having the goal of $1 Million by age 60?

I'm confident in saying, without your goal, your net worth would have been nowhere close to $900,000. Great job! Sometimes, getting close, is good enough! Have faith!

You can do this! Just take it one day at a time.

CHAPTER 15:
CHANGING CAREERS

"I'm Proud to Be an American, where at least I know I'm free"
- Lee Greenwood

To my Brothers and Sisters in Arms, thank you
for your loyal service to our Country.

Making the transition to civilian life will require a few adjustments. In addition to using everything in this guide to give yourself a competitive advantage, I recommend that you;

Change how you talk:

Drop the *Sir*, and *Hooah* and all the military jargon and pick up the jargon of your new profession. Change your voicemail; delete all military references and make it professional. Drop the phrase, *in the military...* Instead use, *in the past...* When answering a phone just say, *Hello*.

Change how you look:

Let your hair grow longer. Stay physically fit. Invest in some nice clothing; no shiny shoes or buttons on your lapel.

Change your resume:

Stop listing what you were responsible for; no one cares. List what you and your unit achieved, maintained, or exceeded based upon the military's *Band of Excellence* (BOE). Use transferrable skills like led, managed, directed, supervised, coordinated, and facilitated and list the details: # people involved, degree of difficulty, problems resolved, BOE, recognition received. Add security clearance. Civilians are associates, team members or employees, not personnel.

Example: Instead of, *Responsible for deploying an Infantry Platoon to Iraq,*

> Add, *Led a 25-member team that moved from Texas to Iraq, with 9 vehicles (plus weapons, radios, ...), traveling 500 miles via rail to Galveston, 3700 miles via ship to Kuwait, and 450 miles via convoy to our desert base in Iraq, ready to accomplish our security mission, with no accidents, injuries, or loss of equipment, all in 21 days.*

When your resume's done, ask a non-military person (not your spouse) to read it to see if he understands it. Then, get it on LinkedIn, Monster, and Career Builder.

Change how you search:

Search the web for companies that hire/assist in the placement/recruiting of former military. Stay in touch with all your military peers and superiors via LinkedIn.com. You may need them as a reference later and you have no idea where they'll be working after they leave the military.

But, always keep…

- The military *values* you acquired during the time you served

- Your sense of *duty* and *commitment* to something greater than yourself

- Your ability to *make things happen* under difficult circumstances

Focus on your future:

Use the Post 9/11 GI Bill to fund additional education and training (like certifications, licenses, and computer skills like MS Project) that you can add to your resume to make you more marketable. If you don't have a college degree, get one. If you have one, get an MBA. You earned your benefits - now use them!

THE END!

Congratulations! You've reached the end of this book. Thank you for reading! Please remember to share what you have learned with others. If you help others succeed, they'll return the favor.

This book focused on *How to Choose the Career You Were Meant to Have.* If you found this book of value, you'll also find value in the other books from *The Effectiveness Guide* series (see Other Books).

The subjects covered will enhance your career by teaching you how to become absolutely essential to any organization and how to become more effective tomorrow than you are today.

You can do this! I have faith in you. What's holding you back?

Self-Assessment:

After reading this book:

- How can you use what you've learned to become more effective tomorrow than you are today?

- How can you use it to become absolutely essential and irreplaceable to any employer?

- How can you use it outside of work (in your community, church, or home) to become better?

- Who else could use it to help them become better?

Do something meaningful with your life. Pay it forward.
Help someone else rise.

ACKNOWLEDGEMENTS

*"Many people will walk in and out of your life, but only
true friends will leave footprints in your heart."*
- Eleanor Roosevelt

I'd like to recognize those with whom I've had the pleasure of serving, whose Leadership and Character I vividly recall, many of whom are not here today to tell their story.

For my military career, I thank Betty McInte, Edward J. Murphy (my Dad), Dale R. Nelson, Geoffrey "Jeff" Prosch, Craig "Randy" Rutler, Dave Wagner, John Andrews, John "The Bear" Warren, John "Jack" Costello, Dan Labin, and Ron Nicholl for their example of Effective Leadership.

*To my fellow Brothers and Sisters-in-Arms, I thank you
for your faithful service to our nation, especially those
who have fallen in the line-of-duty.*

Special thanks to my long-time mentor and friend, Joyce Kuntz, who encouraged me to write this book. After leaving the US Military, Joyce was my first and best employer when I joined her consulting firm in Seattle years ago. Joyce is gone now, but her legacy lives on in this book.

*"I must be able to say with sincerity that to see things differently is a
strength, not a weakness, in my relationship with others."*
- Joyce Kuntz

I thank Joyce's husband, Ed Kuntz, who turned out to be the man who brought me to Seattle from Kansas City, to start my incredible second career as an Executive Coach.

For my coaching career, I thank Tony Robbins, Bernard Haldane, Jack Bissell, Len Drew, Wayne McCullum, Bob Schrier, John Hurtig, and Bob Gerberg for their mentoring and coaching.

I thank my Nephew, Rob Chase, for creating the superb cover graphics and his sound advice along the way.

I thank my editors, Adriane Hesselbein, Terri Beard, Lance Revo, Dan Labin, Dennis Cavin, Bill O'Donnell, Andrew Potter, and Kevin Hughes, who did a great job helping me make this book more understandable and useful.

A special thanks to my two dear friends, partners, and co-authors, Lee Lacy and Jason Bowne, who continue to support me in this worthwhile effort.

For all those whose names are not found here, rest assured that you are not forgotten. Your legacy lives on in my heart and in this book because of your immeasurable contributions to my life. This book is for you.

And, finally, I thank my soul-mate and wife, ***Diana,*** for her love, encouragement and understanding throughout this process.

When I count my blessings, I always count her twice.

ABOUT THE FOUNDER

"I expect to pass through this world but once; any good thing therefore that I can do, or any kindness that I can show to any fellow creature, let me do it now; let me not defer or neglect it, for I shall not pass this way again." - Stephan Grelle

Ed Murphy considers himself lucky. From age 7, he knew what he wanted to be when he grew up. He wanted to be a Soldier. In 1964, four days after graduating from High School, he joined the US Army and found himself in Basic Training and Advanced Infantry Training at Fort Dix, New Jersey.

A year later, Ed became a Cadet at the United States Military Academy at West Point. In 1970, he graduated as a 2d Lieutenant headed to Airborne and Ranger School, then off to Viet Nam for a year.

In 1978, Ed returned to West Point to teach Military Science and earned a Master's Degree from Long Island University in night school. His greatest achievement during his time in the military was helping 1400 soldiers begin their college education during his last two years in West Germany as a Battalion Commander. He wanted to give his soldiers something of real value - something that no one could ever take away. After 23 years as a US Army Officer, from Viet Nam to Desert Storm, he retired in 1993.

Ed then decided, with a little help from *Anthony Robbins*, that his second career would be as an Executive Coach. For the next 21 years, he worked for four of the largest consulting, outplacement and e-cruiting companies in America from Seattle, San Diego, to Kansas City.

In 2012, Ed retired a second time and decided to document everything he learned from those he admired and willingly followed over his 50+ years in both the US Military as an Army Officer and Corporate America as an Executive Coach. Since many of them aren't alive today to tell their stories, he wanted to pay tribute to them before their lessons were lost forever. Thanks to them, he's collected thousands of small and simple things (tactics, techniques, and tools) that have helped and will continue to help future generations to maximize their true career potential by becoming more effective at work and in life.

In 2014, Ed created *TheCAREERMaker.com*, a site dedicated to providing the best-in-class wisdom, knowledge, and advice on how to maximize your true career potential by teaching three simple things; how to become absolutely essential and irreplaceable to any leader, how to become more effective tomorrow than you are today, and how to find and build the career you were meant to have. His greatest joy comes from helping others avoid or overcome the problems he's faced during his lifetime.

In 2016, with the help of two partners and co-authors *Lee O. Lacy and Jason Bowne*, he finally completed *The Effectiveness Guide*, which teaches how to become more effective tomorrow than you are today by consistently producing excellent results; treating others with dignity, respect, and kindness; and helping others to do the same.

Today, Ed considers himself fortunate to get to live in Phoenix, AZ, where he enjoys writing, eating sushi, genealogy, and watching movies with family, friends, and his best friend and wife, *Diana*.

OTHER BOOKS

THESE BOOKS WILL TEACH YOU HOW TO MAXIMIZE YOUR TRUE CAREER POTENTIAL AND ARE AVAILABLE FROM ALL MAJOR ONLINE BOOK RETAILERS

If you liked this book, you'll really like the others in our collection.

From *The Effectiveness Guide* series, topics include:

Volume 1: Your Guide to Better Followership

Volume 2: Your Guide to Better Delegating

Volume 3: Your Guide to Better Planning

Volume 4: Your Guide to Better Organizing

Volume 5: Your Guide to Better Communicating

Volume 6: Your Guide to Better Problem-Solving & Decision-Making

Volume 7: Your Guide to Better Awareness

Volume 8: Your Guide to Better Training

Volume 9: Your Guide to Better Motivating

Volume 10: Your Guide to Better Character

Volume 11: The Effectiveness Guide (includes Volumes 1-10)

Volume 12: Make It Happen! How to Manage Projects

Volume 13: Your Guide to Better Credibility with Your Leader

From *The Career Potential* series, topics include:

- Finding a New Job in 90 Days or Less

- Choosing a Career That Matters

- Interview Like You Mean It

- Does Your Resume Make Your Phone Ring?

- Negotiating Total Compensation

- 19+ Proven Ways to Get Your Resume to the Right People

- Changing Your Career?

- Getting THE Call for Job Interviews and Offers

All the above books are also available from our Book Store at *TheCareerMaker.com*.

ONE LAST THING...

Finally, if you feel this information could help someone else, please take a few moments to let them know. If it turns out to make a difference in their life, they'll be forever grateful to you – as will I.

Let's make a difference together - one person at a time!

All the best!

Founder of *TheCAREERMaker.com*

Coauthor of *The Effectiveness Guide*

email: ed.murphy77@gmail.com

Stop wishing you were better and do something about it today!

INDEX

www.ingramcontent.com/pod-product-compliance
Lightning Source LLC
Chambersburg PA
CBHW070811180526
45168CB00002B/576